CASSIUS CLAY: A Biography

HAMMAD IS HIS APOSTLE

Signing autographs at a Muslim gathering

(Photo: Lee Balterman)

CASSIUS CLAY

A Biography

JACK OLSEN

PELHAM BOOKS

First published in Great Britain by
PELHAM BOOKS LTD
26 *Bloomsbury Street*
*London, W.C.*1
1967

© 1967 *by Jack Olsen*

*Set and printed in Great Britain by Tonbridge Printers Ltd, Peach
Hall Works, Tonbridge, Kent, in Garamond twelve on thirteen point,
and bound by James Burn at Esher, Surrey*

For Su

ILLUSTRATIONS

Signing autographs at a Muslim gathering *frontispiece*

A right connects with Floyd Patterson *facing page* 32

Clowning before a fight 33

Cassius Clay in his Miami living-room 64

After driving his bus into a ditch in the
  Catskills 65

Versus Liston, Heavyweight Championship
  bout, Miami, 1964 72

Victory over Liston. Miami, 1964 73

With a Muslim 'sister' 88

'That man, Liston!' 89

With 'mascot' Stepin Fetchit 96

Cassius Clay with Mama 97

Cassius in action against Brian London 128

With the late Malcolm X on the lawn of
  Clay's Miami home 129

Cassius at home 136

Angelo Dundee, Clay and William Faversham 137

Cassius singing with the late Sam Cooke 152

A champion's smile 153

What strange times we live in. What a strange, uncommon man is Clay. Who can fathom him? We can only watch in wonder as he performs and ponder whether, despite his often truly affecting ways, he doesn't scorn us and the world he is champion of.

GILBERT ROGIN

Part One

IT IS ONE OF THOSE HOUSES THAT ALWAYS SEEM STUFFY, where the warm smell of dinner hangs around the next morning and you can reconstruct the previous night's menu by sniffing in corners. In this house in a shabby section of north-west Miami, there is the constant presence of Negroes, of too many humans for the size of the place, whatever their colour. They drift in and out: celebrity Negroes, little children Negroes, big sparring-partner Negroes, door-to-door salesman Negroes, neatly dressed Muslim Negroes, quick-dollar Negroes, old Negroes in skinny yellow shoes, young Negroes in pork-pie hats, affluent Negroes driving black Cadillacs. In this house, kept neat and tidy by three uniformed Muslim 'sisters', there remains something of the atmosphere of a 'coloured only' waiting-room on the main line of the Florida East Coast Railroad.

One afternoon in the early spring of 1966 a nine-passenger black Cadillac pulled up on the sandy shoulder in front of the house and disgorged Cassius Marcellus Clay, also known as Muhammad Ali, the heavyweight champion of the world; his brother Rudolph, also known as Rahman Ali; Clay's bodyguard, Sam Saxon, also known as Cap'n Sam; Clay's driver and handyman, Reggie, also known as 'Hey', and assorted other Negroes. In the wake of the big black car came several others, remoras trying to keep up with the shark: a few journalists, hanging on Muhammad's every word; two or three big men about 'spooktown', as Muhammad calls the horribly run-down Negro slum of Miami; a white man who wanted to sell the champion a house, a coloured man who wanted to sell him some purses, and a few others. When all were assembled inside the little living-room, Clay wasted no time in launching into his afternoon sermon. 'Well, boys, I have something to tell you,' he said by way of attracting total attention. Anything less than total attention always annoys Cassius. A hush fell on the room, broken only by the occasional clink of a pot from the adjoining kitchen, whence runaway wisps of steam evidenced the activities of the three Muslim sisters, preparing their strange admixtures for dinner, using items like caraway and sesame seeds and carrot fluff and okra. 'I've now been champion of the world for two years and the day I won that title—' The champion interrupted himself, as is his practice. 'Rahman, bring those bunch of films out!' Rudolph Clay, a study in sibling obedience, was on his feet at the word 'Rahman' and half-way into the next room at the word 'films'. 'You are very lucky men to be here with the heavyweight champion,' Clay said to the assemblage, 'listening to him recite his poems and make smart remarks.'

There was a mumbled chorus of 'oh yehs' and 'yes sirs', and one little round man sitting in the corner said, 'A real honour, a real honour . . .'

'Yeh, my man,' Cassius said in his wavery-quavery 'preacher' voice, 'we pushing the last days now. I been predicting and predicting and predicting, popping off and popping off and popping off, writing poems and writing poems and writing poems, hollering and hollering and hollering, and now it's the end of the line.' The uninitiated leaned forward in their seats, astonished to be in the presence of history on the fly, wondering what pronouncement was going to follow. The end of the line?

12

Was he retiring? Older hands sat back and waited for Clay's mood to change. They knew that he could announce his retirement at lunchtime and discuss plans for another fight over postlunch coffee, then retire again at dinnertime and come out of retirement by midnight. But no matter how bored they might have been by Clay's free-wheeling monologue, everyone feigned interest. It is required. Clay has been known to turn on sullen reporters and say, 'Hey, why ain't you taking notes on all this?' and on friends and say, 'Why ain't you laughing?' Full attention is the rule at all times.

'Every one of my predictions have come true,' Cassius said. 'The world is now bowing to the fact that I am the greatest. There are no challenges around. I have been so powerful and so accurate in my predictions that I must now stay silent to keep the world from not coming to my fights. I must stay silent to keep the people, for if I talk they will believe it. If I say I am going to knock somebody out in one round, they are going to believe it and they are not going to come to my fight. If I predict, they will believe it, so the only thing I can capitalise on and continue are my great poems. I have become so popular at my poetry and my styling until anyone associated with me becomes world famous. After they break up with me, they write for top magazines, they are put on top TV shows. I am so popular that movie plays about boxing are outlined around many of my ways. There was a TV play the other night and this Negro walked into a bar and this white fellow was there and this Negro says, "I been looking for you, you got to fight me because you see, man, I'm beautiful." He said, "Don't nobody touch me, because I'm beautiful!"'

There were 'oooOOOs' and 'my mys' and 'don't says' from the audience and, thus encouraged, Cassius repeated the story three times and the phrase 'I'm beautiful' eight times, and each time the audience reacted as though the story were brand-new. Mercifully, Sam Saxon had finished threading the home movie projectors, and now he began rolling the first film presentation of the sultry afternoon: the Cassius Clay–Doug Jones fight, an odd choice to set before the king, since it showed Clay at his early, amateurish worst, hamming around the ring, getting stunned by a vicious right hand, failing to solve Jones' journeyman defences, and winning a decision that many ringsiders felt should have gone to the hard-working but unglamorous Jones. Just before the film began, Clay recited:

> I was talking with a loud tone
> The night I met Mr Jones.
> They say he was rough
> And they say he was tough,
> But to beat Ali it wasn't enough.

The fight film had hardly started before brother Rudolph was screaming and hollering like a fan at ringside. 'Oh, you cooked! You cooked on him!'

'Steamroll him!' Sam Saxon cried.

'As you see,' Cassius said,

> I dance and I have a fast hook.
> I take the people's money like I'm a crook.

In between rounds, while the cheering crowd in the tiny living-room got its breath (what little breath was available in the close quarters), Cassius reminded one and all: 'You fellows are awful lucky to be here today with the heavyweight champion and all his friends.'

Round two began and Rudolph shouted, 'Look at that fast punching! Heavyweights just don't punch like that!'

'Look at how low I hold my guard,' Cassius said. 'I'm the onliest fighter alive can hold their guard that low and get away with it.'

As the fight film wore on, ten rounds of flailing and jabbing and missed opportunities by both fighters, the living-room fight crowd grew more and more lively, with the spectators seeming to vie for the honour of showing the most enthusiasm and knowledgeability about the superiority of the young Clay. Rudy soon abandoned all his dignity for a series of war cries and whoops. It was not easy to figure out what he was whooping about; he reminded one of little old grandmothers who attend their first fight and imagine that every slipped punch, every missed roundhouse right and every flashy bolo is a score. 'He was born a champion!' Rudy said between cries.

'Stomp on him!' said Saxon, as the two fighters exchanged wild and meaningless hooks. 'Stomp on him!'

'Whoo-eeee!' cried Rudolph. 'Whoo-EEEE! He was born to fight! He was fighting from the cradle!'

Clay brushed Jones with a left hook on the little screen and Saxon said, 'Look at that, Ali! You hit him with the kitchen sink and he's still hanging! You had to be a good man to whup Jones that night, Ali.'

Clay landed a series of light jabs and the crowd in the room acted as though they were sharing the pain from the awful blows. *Ooooooooohhhhhh! Owwwwwwwwww! Ohhhhhhhhhh!* 'Man, his eye's bleeding!' somebody shouted over the sound effects. 'The blows is falling off Jones like raindrops.' Clay's jabs kept popping into the vicinity of Jones' face, most of them landing on his gloves and arms, but the faithful retainers went wild. The screams and shouts in the room reached a crescendo, and Rudy led the pack, making a cry like a wolfhound opening on a trail. Somebody cried, *'Yip! yip! yip!'* and when the final bell rang, Sam Saxon said quickly, 'Look at that! Jones won the first round and that's all. I know! I studied it!' There were loud arguments on just how big Clay had won the fight, and the consensus was that Cassius took all rounds except possibly one. Homage thus dutifully rendered, the group sat back to hear from Himself, who obliged in a high, sing-song voice: 'Mu-ham-mad A-li, the greatest fighter that there will *ever* will be!' Then he recited in its entirety an early paean of self-praise, while the assemblage clucked in admiration of the lyric sweep and metre of the lines. A big laugh was enjoyed by all when Clay concluded: 'If Cassius says a mosquito can pull a plough, don't ask how. Hitch him up!' He winked at two reporters present, said 'You're gonna have something good, something exclusive, to go back with,' and began a 'new' poem about a presumably forthcoming fight with Ernie Terrell. The poem turned out to be remarkably similar to an earlier effort about Sonny Liston. Cassius recited:

Clay comes out to meet Terrell and Terrell starts to retreat.
If Terrell goes back an inch farther he'll end up in a ringside seat.
Clay swings with a left, Clay swings with a right.
Just look at young Cassius carry the fight.
Terrell keeps backing but there's not enough room.
It's a matter of time until Clay lowers the boom.
Then Clay lands with a right – what a beautiful swing.
And the punch raised Terrell clear out of the ring.
Terrell is still risin' and the ref wears a frown,
But he can't start counting until Terrell comes down.
Now Terrell disappears from view; the crowd is getting frantic.
But our radar stations have picked him up somewhere over the Atlantic.
Who on earth thought when they came to the fight
That they would witness the launching of a human satellite?

The original poem was the same word for word, except, of course, for the insertion of Liston for Terrell, and two extra lines at the end:

Yes, the crowd did not dream when they laid down their money
That they would see a total eclipse of the Sonny.

'Now,' Clay said, when the applause had died, 'I am prepared to reveal the round when I will defeat Terrell, but only to the highest bidder. If you offer me a couple thousand, I might tell you the round. Maybe eight or nine rounds, that kinda prediction won't hurt the gate. I got a prediction for you fellows, but you *must* pay.'

'Should we start the bidding at around fifty thousand dollars?' asked Mort Sharnik of *Sports Illustrated*, but the gentle sarcasm was lost on Clay, who seldom hears anything that is said to him, especially if it is funny.

'Now I am going to tell you all a joke,' Clay said, and immediately brother Rudolph began laughing.

'I just know this gonna be so funny,' Rudolph said, struggling to contain himself.

'Sammy Davis, Jr, went up to see Lyndon Johnson,' Cassius began, 'and he said, "LBJ, if you let me run for Vice-President in the next election, I can guarantee you'll win the election for the next four years." And Johnson said, "How do you mean that?" And Sammy Davis, Jr, said: "Four reasons." ' A newcomer, sparring partner James Ellis, walked into the room, so Cassius took the joke from the top. ' " . . . Four reasons",' he said finally. ' "Number one, I'm Jewish. You'll get all the Jewish vote. Number two, I'm a Negro and you'll get all the Negro votes. Number three, my wife is Scandinavian and you'll get all the Scandinavian votes. Number four, you'll have the greatest life insurance and the greatest protection and security that any President has ever had." Johnson said, "How you mean that?" And Sammy Davis, Jr, he said, "Who in the hell gonna kill you knowing a Negro gonna be the next President?" '

At first there was a confused silence, but when everyone realised the joke was over, a loud caterwauling went up. Rudolph knelt on the floor. Sam Saxon held his sides and claimed to be in pain.

'Hold on for another one,' Cassius said, jumping in to

exploit his advantage over the group, now at the mercy of his rapier wit. 'This man and his girl friend went to a masquerade party, and the girl wore a cow outfit, head and body just like a cow, and the man wore a bull outfit, and they were driving and the car stopped when they ran out of gas and she said, "Oh, what are we gonna do?" and he said, "Oh, we're just a mile from the party, we'll cut across the field." So they cut across the field and they ran into a real bull. And she say, 'Oh, honey, what are we gonna do?" and he say, "I don't know 'bout you, but I'm gonna eat some grass. *You* better brace yo'self!" ' A hurricane of laughter shook the room. 'You better brace yo'self!' Cassius said at the first sign of abatement, whereupon the appreciation of his humour broke out again. Finally quiet returned, and Cassius squeezed out one last round of chuckles by saying, 'Yeah, and he say, "You better brace yo'self!" '

Sam Saxon had made ready another film, a BBC interview which had been conducted in the back seat of Clay's big Cadillac as it cruised about town. There were cries of assent in the room when the BBC interviewer asked Clay why he needed a nine-passenger automobile and Cassius answered: 'All big people have chariots . . . I am king of the whole world. I really need ten or fifteen of these things.' Clay watched the film appreciatively from his seat on the couch, as though he were looking at a world premiere, as though he had not seen this particular film at least fifty times before.

'Some day,' he said, when the filmed interview was over, 'I'm gonna put all this together for my little children. I'm gonna pay a camera crew to follow me and film me all day the day of the fight. They'll record my conversation around the room, me sleeping, getting in the car, going to the fight. You know what I should have? I should have two girls with me to work those court reporter machines and follow me all the time and tape everything that happens . . . '

Abruptly his mood appeared to change. His voice grew tired and soft, and a slow, ministerial cadence came into it. 'Yes, sir,' he said, 'I remember my training days, building gates, working hard, working too hard. My old campaign days . . . Now I don't have to campaign no more. I'm getting tired, and I'm getting old.' He began a kind of sing-song chant, running along on a level tone and dropping down three or four notes in pitch on the last word of each phrase:

> Training is getting
>> hard.
> Getting up and running is getting
>> hard.
> I really don't know what to
>> dooooooooooo.
> Listen while I talk to you.

This last line being the first line of a song, he slipped quickly into the tune. 'Listen while I talk to you . . . There's a new dance a-going 'round. Let me tell you what I'm putting down.' He sang well, like a Nat Cole disciple. 'Shake, oh, pretty baby, shake. That's the way to dooooooooooo it. Shake Ooooh, ooooh, ooooh, shake it like a bowl of soup!'

Two little girls in droopy drawers appeared at the front door, and Cassius quickly broke off his recital. 'Oh, somebody open that door and let those little girls come in,' he ordered. 'Open that door quick! Come here, girls! Come here, girl! Come here, Tanya. That your name, Tanya?' The little girl, about four, climbed on his lap. 'Oh, *Tandra*,' he said. 'Where's my hug? Where's my kiss?' He beckoned to the other girl, who was about two. 'Don't you go nowhere, girls.' He nuzzled them both, making snorting noises like a hog rooting for food. The little girls laughed and put their arms around him. 'Where you been, girls? Over to the neighbours' house? I haven't seen you in *so* long. How you been doing? All right, huh? All right, you gonna give me a big hug before you go? How's your mama and daddy? All right? That's good. Okay, be good girls!' They ran out the door.

'Hey, Cap'n,' Cassius said, 'put on that colour film about me . . . me and the car. Yes, sir, in living colour from Hollywood, California, in his first major movie, Muhammad Ali in *The Dragon Return from the Green Lagoon*. Muhammad Ali stars in the star role, *dum dum dum. Pum pum pump pump pum*.' He called toward the kitchen: 'What all are you cooking, sisters? Steak! Salad! Baked potatoes? String beans? *Carrot fluff!* OoooEEEE, string beans and carrot fluff . . . '

'Ladies and gentlemen,' he said, when the colour film began, 'this is now the great Muhammad Ali cruising through Santa Monica, California. Now this is Miami Beach. The heavyweight champ of the world could live here if he wants to. This could be his pool if he wanted it. He could be driving his Cadillac to his own one-hundred-thousand-dollar home if he wanted to. "Where's Muhammad Ali?" they'll say, and I'll say, "I'm out there integrating that pool."' For a while he continued his mental ramble, like a latter-day Leopold Bloom, throwing in snatches of song, poems, tributes to his skills. 'When I fight Terrell in Chicago,' he said, anticipating an event which came off early in February, 1967, 'we'll fill up the place, right, Sam?'

'If we can take a little country town like Lewiston, Maine,' Sam said, 'and draw people from everywhere, and out in the desert in Las Vegas we can draw a great big old house, think about what we'll draw in Chicago. Chicago gonna be red hot. *Gonna be red hot!* The whole country gonna be smoking that night.'

'Everybody can get to Chicago,' Cassius said, 'and there's a lot of people live there, too.'

Sam said, 'That's the centre of America.'

Rudolph joined in. 'That's a good place. That's a good place. Right in the centre. Right in the centre of America.' Rudolph has a tendency, perhaps picked up from his father, to repeat himself.

'You think Chicago'll be sold out a week before the fight?' Cassius asked.

Sam said, 'Them pimps gonna buy up all the seats. Pimps and hustlers. See, they ain't got nowhere to go now.'

Cassius nodded his agreement. A few more remarks were ignored by him; Cassius had decided to tell one more racial joke, and he was honing it to dramatic sharpness in his mind. 'Just a minute,' he said. 'Okay, now pay attention. Have you all heard of Yuma, Arizona? Do you know how it got the name?'

Nobody knew how Yuma had got its name.

'This big Negro cowboy was riding through Yuma, Arizona, before they named it in 1804.' He paused to let Rudolph's laughter subside. 'He's riding through Yuma, Arizona.' Again he paused while Rudolph cackled and said, 'Oh, this gonna be *so* funny!'

Cassius resumed: 'And you know how people say that most Negroes' favourite curse word is "you mothafucka? You mothafucka?" And let me tell you something, this Negro cowboy was riding through Arizona and he was on a white horse and he had on a red hat and a pink outfit and two gold guns. He was a bad cat, and he says, "I'll stop in this old town and get me a beer, there's an old saloon over there." ' Cassius interrupted the monologue to do his own excellent impression of the horse's hoofs and the horse's whinnying as the cowboy pulled him up. Rudy wiped the tears from his eyes and said, 'Oh, he's something else, something else!' as though he were about to succumb to hysteria.

'And then he walked in the bar,' Cassius went on, 'and

they said, "No niggers allowed in the front. Go in the back!" So he walked on to the back and got a cold beer and got drunk, and he said, "I'm going back in the front." He went around and kicked the door in, and he said, "I'm the baddest gun in the world! What chew mean no niggers in the front door?"

'Wild Bill Elliot was sitting over in the corner and he said, "Back on out that door!"

'And the Negro he say, "Just shoot me down." He says, "Call your play!" He says, "Ain't no man in the world can beat me drawing." He says, "I'm coming in here and I'm gonna be the first Negro to drink a beer in here," and the Negro went to get his gun and Wild Bill Elliot shot him—*pow! pow!*—and the Negro say, 'You mo— You mo—" And then he fall daid.

'And that's how they named Yuma, Arizona. You mo— Yu-ma. Get it?'

Everybody got it, and everybody laughed.

Later Cassius fell to talking about childhood, a favourite subject. He feels that he is one of the masters of the art of reminiscence, and often spins long stories about pre-school years simply to impress listeners with his memory. 'I can remember walking down Thirty-second Street,' he said. 'We got off the bus at Thirty-second and Greenwood and walked over a block to Grand and it was a cold winter day, a cool spring evening. Me, my mother, my father and my brother. I was about four, three and a half. That's a good memory, huh? And my daddy was carrying my brother in his arms and I was holding my mother's hand. And I remember when there was a little white girl lived down the street from us and we used to run up and down the alley and play all the time with her. There was a big garage in the back, and my daddy used to make toys all the time and put 'em up in this big two-storey garage, used to make dolls and horses and waggons, like milkmen's waggons with the horses with it, and all of that, and I used to go up there and hunt for toys, and I remember my mother doing exercises on the floor. I said, "Mama, what're you doing?" and she said she just keep trim, lose weight, used to bend over and touch her toes.' Inspired by the memories of his mama, he picked up the phone and after three hurried attempts at the direct long-distance dialling managed to reach his parents' home in the outskirts of Louisville, Kentucky.

'How you feel, Bird?' he asked, using his childhood name for his mother, Odessa Grady Clay, who, in turn, calls Cassius 'Gee' or 'Gee Gee', in memory of the first words he ever uttered. None of that Muhammad Ali stuff for Odessa Clay, or for her husband, Cassius Clay, Sr, for that matter. 'I'm here in Florida training, Bird. How you feeling? . . . That's good, that's my sweet mama . . . You know sumpin? I was talking about where we used to live. Hey, Mama, you remember we used to live out there next to Churchill Downs? Yeh, Heywood Street, it's still there, ain't it? . . . I remember it . . . Didn't you used to do exercises, bend over and touch your toes and things?' He laughed twice, a deep mellow laugh, at his mother's answer. 'Uh huh . . . Um hmmmmmm . . . You remember a boy named Rudolph used to go out there and park cars for people?' As the two rambled on about his childhood, all of the pretender seemed to fall away from Cassius, and he became a young boy talking to his mother, laughing, sharing interlocking memories. In conversation with his mother, he seemed most like a real person, with a genuinely integrated personality. 'You 'member that boy named Bimbo died? . . . How old was I? I was in school, wasn't I? . . . You 'member a little white girl used to live around there we used to run around and play with? And a dark girl named Penny next door? She was living for a while and then one day somebody said Penny died.' His voice reflected the contentment that comes to an adult when he talks to a parent about the days when life was simple, the days before responsibility and confusion. Beyond that simple satisfaction of reliving the past, Cassius seemed to feel that it was time and money well spent to prove with his mother the earliest minutes of his life, as though the sheer magnitude of the subject justified the bother, like a biographer researching Baudelaire. He discussed the smallest matters in infinite detail. One day in the distant past somebody had broken a chair on Heywood Street, and mother and son spent long-distance-rate minutes trying to figure out who had broken it, what kind of chair it had been, where Cassius had been when the incident occurred. 'Now say hello to Rudy, Bird,' Clay said at last. 'Don't I remember a lot, Mama?'

Rudolph took over the phone. 'Hello, Mama . . . Fine, fine . . . Yes, ma'am . . . How's Daddy? . . . We'll see yeh at the fight in Chicago . . . Me and Gee'll be back in Chicago for the [Muslim] convention and I'll drive down and get y'all if you'd like to come to the convention.' It was a peculiar remark for Rudolph to make. He knew that neither of his parents would go near a Muslim convention, both of them having gone on record with violently anti-Muslim sentiments that nearly sundered the family. But Rudolph, an ardent Muslim, evidently never tired of trying to bring his parents into the fold. 'If the weather's not too bad I'll run down and get you . . . Yeah, her and her mother both told me to give you their love, Bird . . . They think you're a darling, a wonderful person . . . Okay, baby, we think you're as sweet as you can be . . . Yes, ma'am, we think you're sweet . . . Okay, baby, I'm writing her now and I'll tell her, hear? Now give Daddy our love and our regards, hear? And y'all just take it easy . . . Y'all be sweet . . . How you feeling? You got any pain? [Mrs Clay had undergone surgery for ulcers] . . . Any pain at all? . . . Oh, that's good. And you lost thirteen pounds? Yes, ma'am, I'll tell her. Yes, ma'am . . . Okay, baby . . . All right, baby, you lost thirteen pounds . . . Okay, sweet baby . . . I'm gonna kiss you when I see you, sweet baby . . . '

Listening to the brothers Clay at their end of the telephone, one could not help feeling that one had caught them at their most human, at their most real, at a second in their lives when they were exposing a certain inner sweetness of character. It was a rare moment, a kind of epiphany, seldom to be enjoyed by outsiders.

In a tiny front bedroom of the small bungalow, the world's heavyweight champion lay half awake, undergoing an interview about his early life, trying not to tell too much, partially because there are portions that are painful to him and partially because he is under the impression that his 'whole life story, as told by me myself,' is a precious commodity worth a minimum of $50,000. Clay gives away little that he can sell. The telephone rang on the cluttered dresser next to the bed, and the champion, in his role as Muhammad Ali, picked it up and said a dignified 'Hello.' The caller was a local television personality, a man who could generate some publicity; so Cassius loosened up. 'Hello, Mis-ter Ed Lane,' he said cheerfully. This is one of Clay's trademarks: calling white men by both their names. He likes to spot them approaching, and when they come into range, he beams and throws out with mock pomposity and careful syllabication: 'An-ge-lo Dun-dee!' 'Gor-don Da-vid-son!' 'Gil-bert Ro-gin!' That is, if he remembers the name. It takes many exposures to a white man before his name sinks into the consciousness of Cassius Clay. A white man's name is of no importance to him, nor are 'Whiteys' themselves, except insofar as they can further his career. Mr Ed 'Mark 'Em Down' Lane, an old acquaintance who sold cars and conducted conversational television interviews over a Miami station, fell in this latter category. 'How you feeling?' Cassius asked. Whatever Lane replied, Cassius began one of his patented Greek-chorus speeches, a mock lament that sounded as though it had been written the night before, rehearsed for several hours and saved for just such an auspicious occasion as a telephone call from Mr Ed 'Mark 'Em Down' Lane. 'I stay in the paper, don't I?' Cassius said softly into the phone. 'Poor old me. Always in the press. Man, man! What do people *think* about me? A young, twenty-four-year-old boy, just an athlete, in the headlines eight times out of ten for something other than boxing and always something controversial, exciting and drama. Year in, year out. Month after month, never dies, and I manage to come through it all still strong, and trained, too. What *do* people think about me?'

The insinuation, of course, was that people thought he was a marvel, a wonder, a blessing to the boxing world, a credit to his race and to all mankind. Cassius Clay, insulated and isolated in his cocoon of yes-men and hero-worshippers, is capable of believing that people feel the same admiration for him that he has for himself, that the whole world would laugh at his jokes and be struck dumb by his skills, even as his flunkeys in Miami were. But the fact is that public opinion toward Cassius, even then, had already curdled. The trouble included his first Army tests, which he took in 1964. Clay passed everything physical, but he was a failure in the mental testing. According to Stephen Ailes, then Secretary of the Army, Clay was 'given additional testing and psychological evaluations to determine if he was a true or deliberate failure . . . and it was determined by the personnel psychologist that Clay was a true failure and gave no evidence of malingering.'

A clamour arose. People wanted to know how a big, strong kid like Cassius, with a flair for writing poetry and a knack for public relations, could be mentally unfit for military service. 'Hell, there's lots of things he could do in the Army,' said a Miami critic of the champion. 'Does he need a high I.Q. to drive garbage trucks, sort mail, peel potatoes, scrub out pots and pans? Holy Moses, they got guys in the Army stupider than he is. One of 'em was my colonel!'

Ailes reviewed the record and decided that the best course was to have Cassius examined again, 'to eliminate any element of doubt as to his true mental ability and the possibility that anxiety about his forthcoming title fight [with Liston] might have influenced his test scores.' The second battery of tests was administered in Louisville with a senior psychologist on hand to observe and report directly to the Secretary. Clay came out of the testing room wringing wet after two and a half hours of rigorous examination. 'That test was tough,' he said. 'Tougher than the first one. Man, I am tired, but I did my best. I don't want anybody to think I'm crazy. I remember one problem went like this: There are twelve bushels of apples. They cost ten dollars each. You buy them, but before you do, you take a third of the apples out of each bushel. How much do you pay for the apples?

'After scratching around ten or fifteen minutes on paper—I never was much good at figuring—I think I got the answer. But then a guy came by, took that test out of my hand and gave me another one. When I looked down on the test he took from me, there still was a whole long row of questions I didn't answer.'

Once again the Army reported that Clay had flunked. The personnel psychologist at the induction station in Louisville studied the whole record, re-interviewed Clay and confirmed 'the original finding of being a true test failure with no evidence of malingering.' Secretary Ailes said the finding 'was supported by Clay's standing in the lowest five per cent of his high school class.' The

Secretary suggested to Rep. Carl Vinson, chairman of the House Armed Services Committee, that *l'affaire* Clay raised two important points: should a man be drafted merely because he is nationally prominent, and are the induction standards too high? 'To accept inductees on the basis of assumed rather than demonstrated ability would risk degrading the combat capability of the Army by inflicting potentially untrainable personnel on it,' Ailes said. 'In my judgment, we must depend on the established standards . . . The requirements of today's Army do not allow for acceptance of those personnel not offering a reasonable value to the defence effort.'

The Secretary's argument made sense to everybody except the general public. Letters were fired off to senators and congressmen and newspapers and television stations, charging that Cassius had perpetrated a brilliant hoax. And the fact that he had not passed two relatively simple mental tests exposed Cassius to an embarrassing public discussion of his intelligence. ('I only said I was the greatest,' he said in response to the outcry. 'I never said I was the smartest.' But people close to him said he was upset by 'all those cats saying I'm stupid, and saying it out loud.') The halls of Congress rang with accusations and counter-accusations on the champion's integrity, and Rep. Frank T. Bow of Ohio demanded a full investigation. Rep. William Bray of Indiana, a member of the House Armed Services Committee, pointed out that there was no inconsistency: Cassius had scored about as well on the Army tests as he had scored on his high school tests. This opened up the subject of Clay's high school education back in Louisville: just how good was it? 'I'll tell you how good it was,' said a native Louisvillian and former high school teacher. 'You can't fire a kid out of the public schools. He's got to stay until he's sixteen, and if he wants to stay on after that, you've got to let him. Now Cassius was the pet at Louisville Central High

School. He was always running off winning Golden Gloves championships and Olympic championships and everything else, and a lot of the time he didn't even show up for classes. They *accommodated* him at Louisville Central. They tried to teach him "boxing mathematics", how to figure gate percentages and income tax stuff and things like that. But otherwise they didn't teach him anything, because they couldn't have; he just wasn't interested in anything but boxing. He graduated almost bottom man in his class with a D minus, and they gave him a diploma. I think they should have just given him a certificate of attendance.'

All sorts of figures were handed out as Clay's intelligence quotient. One report quoted the former principal of Central High School as saying that Cassius had an I.Q. of seventy-eight, ten points below the norm for the school. Another said he had scored ninety. J. Waymond Hackett, who became principal of Central High School after Clay was graduated, said, 'I've seen those published reports and I'm the only one that has access to Clay's real records, and I've got them under lock and key where nobody can see them. But I can tell you that Cassius ought to sue those people that said he had an I.Q. of seventy-eight.'

Clay's personal physician, Dr Ferdie Pacheco, said, 'To label him mentally incompetent for the draft was inaccurate and unrealistic. People lose sight of the fact that some of us do well in a written test and some of us show our intelligence in other ways. Cassius has plenty of intelligence, and if the Army thought otherwise, the Army failed, not Cassius.'

On the other hand, it is evident that Clay is an extremely slow reader, and so poor a writer that a simple letter might take him hours to compose. 'Cassius has trouble writing letters or anything,' Petros M. Spanakos of Brooklyn wrote to the newspaper columnist Red

Smith of the New York *Herald Tribune*. Spanakos, a bantamweight boxer who had been Clay's team-mate in the 1960 Olympic games at Rome, said, 'I spelled out, corrected and finally wrote his letters home. This is why I know C. C. honestly failed the Army I.Q. test that kept him out of the draft.'

Said William Faversham, once Clay's manager and still his friend, 'People say to me, "I don't believe he flunked the Army, I believe the Army didn't want him," and I say, "Well I don't agree." Hell, the night of the Charley Powell fight when Cassius and I were sitting around waiting to get paid off, I said, "Cassius, we can fight Doug Jones in the Garden in March," He said, "Bill, what month is this?" I said, "January." He said, "How many months till March?" He said, "What are we gonna get out of a Jones fight?" I said we'd been guaranteed thirty-five thousand dollars or twenty-five per cent of the gross, whichever was bigger. He said, "Forget about the twenty-five per cent. What would I get out of the guarantee for my half?" I said, "Seventeen thousand five hundred." He couldn't divide thirty-five thousand by two! This went on all the time. "What month is this?" he'd ask me. "How many months is it till February?" And you take something like a newspaper column, a sports column. You and I might read it in three, four minutes. Clay'll take twenty minutes, a half hour. In my opinion, he has no formal education, regardless of what the Louisville school system says.'

Gordon Davidson, a lawyer who was closely associated with Clay from the beginning, spoke out: 'They say the Senate's going to have an investigation of draft deferments and Clay's going to be the first witness they call. Well, if they put him on the stand under oath they'll find out why he was deferred. In about thirty seconds.'

There were still mutterings and grumblings about Clay's deferment when the whole question was rendered moot in 1966 by a new system of classification under which Cassius was immediately rendered 1-A, catching him unawares and making him scream with public pain. 'I don't have nothing against them Viet Congs!' Cassius cried, and within a few days he was being treated like Public Enemy Number One. Newspaper editorial writers and columnists hauled out some of their strongest epithets and hurled them at the surprised Cassius. He was 'a self-centred spoiled brat of a child,' 'a sad apology for a man,' 'the all-time jerk of the boxing world,' 'the most disgusting character in memory to appear on the sports scene,' 'Bum of the month. Bum of the year. Bum of all time.' The governor of Illinois found Clay 'disgusting', and the governor of Maine said Clay should 'be held in utter contempt by every patriotic American'. An American Legion Post in Miami asked people to 'join in condemnation of this unpatriotic, loud-mouthed bombastic individual', and dirty mail began to arrive at Clay's Miami address ('You're nothing but a yellow nigger,' said a typical correspondent, one of many who forgot to sign their names).

The *Chicago Tribune* waged a choleric campaign against holding the next Clay fight in Chicago; the newspaper's attitude seemed to be that thousands of impressionable young Chicagoans would go over to the Viet Cong if Cassius were to be allowed to engage in fisticuffs in that sensitive city. Amplified by the newspaper (on one day it ran eleven items about Clay), the noise became a din, the drumbeats of a holy war. TV and radio commentators, little old ladies from Champaign-Urbana, bookmakers and parish priests, military strategists at the Pentagon and brave dogfeet wading across the ricefields of Vietnam, all joined in a get-Cassius clamour. Just about the only voice raised on behalf of the poor Clay was that of Elijah Muhammad, wispy leader of the Black Muslims, who said rhetorically to the American public: 'You made him a fool. You classified him as unfit and then you call him. You tell him that if he won't go to Vietnam, he can't fight and make money. This is awful! This is a trial!'

There were even a few amateur psychologists who wondered if there might have been more to the public uproar than simple patriotism. 'Doesn't it seem to you that people got madder than they should have?' a friend asked. 'The thing is, Americans have become so guilty about Negroes that they bend over farther than they want to in their attitude toward them. Then along comes somebody like Cassius and they feel free to unload their resentment and pour it on.'

Did he mean that some of the complainants might have been motivated by some factor as evil as race prejudice?

'Well, the people who made the biggest fuss about him are the same ones who blew their tops when he became a Muslim. This made him anti-white and it inflamed their own prejudices. So they could scream about him and what makes it nice is it's so socially acceptable.'

Football star Jimmy Brown, no special admirer of the white race himself, said the real reason for the pressure against Clay was economic. It was indisputably true that white interests were annoyed because Clay had formed a partially Negro organisation, Main Bout, Inc., to handle television income from his fights. Brown, an officer in the group, took his complaints to that old war-horse of race and histrionics, Rep. Adam Clayton Powell, who made the predictable public lament. Clay's remarks about the draft, said the Harlem congressman, 'were no more "unpatriotic", if you want to use that word, and I don't think it is the right word, than the words of Senator Fulbright of Arkansas and Senator Morse of Oregon in their criticism of our Vietnam policy. And they are no more unpatriotic than what I've said myself. I'm a pacifist and Clay, because of his religion, is a pacifist, too.

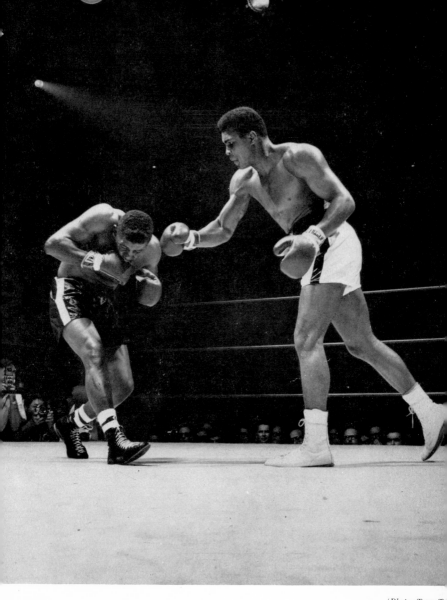

A right connects with Floyd Patterson

(Photo: Tony T·

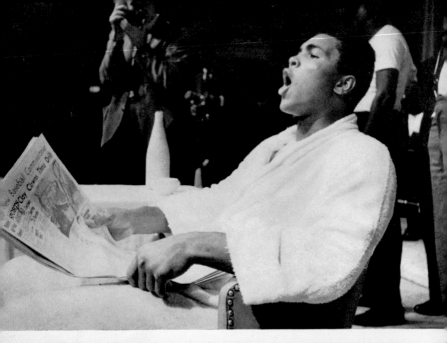

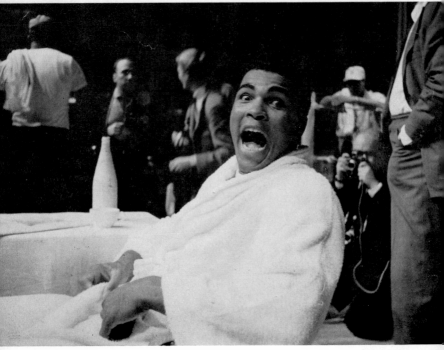

Clowning before a fight

They just don't want to see Negroes cutting up this three-million-dollar melon.'

Whatever the reasons for the national outcry, whether they were racial or economic or just plain superpatriotic, the bombinating Kentucky Negro had rubbed the whole country the wrong way and it had become necessary for the whole country to rise up in anger. As Dr Pacheco explained: 'We're getting back to the Korean War status where the guy who goes into the Army is no longer a jerk but a man who's doing his duty and is to be applauded. Now comes Cassius saying he ain't got nothing against no Viet Congs. Had he come out a year ago with that, many people might have said, 'Well, another Clay witticism.'' Now he says it and he sounds like a traitor, and then he compounds the problem by saying it's a white man's war when there's a lot of coloured people over there dying.'

Said a newspaperman who had studied and enjoyed Clay for six years: 'Every time I begin to think that he really has the makings of a sweet person, he does something like this, something so outrageous. Some of that stuff he's spouting is almost treason. Can you imagine what's gonna happen when he goes in the Army with some sergeant from south Georgia who's had about eight buddies killed in Vietnam?'

Even one of Clay's favourite people, his Aunt Mary Turner, a mathematics teacher in Louisville, spoke out. 'He's gonna mess himself up so won't nobody go see him,' Mrs Turner said with typical Clay-family bluntness. 'Most folks feel like I do: when their sons get ready to go to the Army, they'll just pack the suitcases and go.'

No one who was around Clay during those days when the draft board was getting ready to reclassify him believed that Cassius would 'just pack the suitcases and go.' Clay himself was the most surprised person in Miami when the draft board moved him into 1-A; right up to the moment of the announcement, he had stead-fastly believed that he and the Black Muslims and leader Elijah Muhammad held some sort of power over the government. As Clay confided to a friend, 'They're trying to call me to the Army. Man, they know I ain't going to no Army! They ain't gonna bother me! There's too many people in the world watching me, see, and all of those black people overseas, they're Muslims, they're not Christians. And America's trying to make peace with 'em, and if they give me . . . ' His voice trailed off, and then he resumed his soliloquy in mocking, strident tones: 'But Uncle Sam is a powerful man and when Uncle Sam says Greeeetings, you go! Yeh, man!' His voice turned serious again. 'Yeh, Elijah Muhammad's a powerful man. Whatever he say, goes. Uncle Sam is in wars, wars everywhere, wars all over the country, everybody's at war today . . . ' Now he began an explanation of how he was sacrificing millions of dollars by being a Muslim, but how in the long run he could do more for the cause of the Negro by sticking to his adopted religion and letting the cash go. 'All this stuff I turned down,' he said, 'and I'll show you where it makes me bigger. Look how big I am: I got a call from Washington, the Pentagon called me. They said, "We're not gonna draft you. We've got to fake it because of the public. This has never happened before. We've never had to cope with no one like this before. This is a high office calling!" That's power! They know I'm not going.

'I got invitations now. Haile Selassie want to see me in Ethiopia. That's Moslem country. Ben Bella want to see me in Algeria. King Saud want to see me in Saudi Arabia. King Feisal want to see me in Sudan. President Nasser of Egypt want to see me. These are men own their own countries. Powerful men, man! They own the land, they own millions of acres and control millions of people . . .

34

'The white want me hugging on a white woman, or endorsing some whisky, or some skin bleach, lightening the skin when I'm promoting black as the best . . . They want me advertising all this stuff that'd make me rich but hurt so many others. But by me sacrificing a little wealth I'm helping so many others. Little children can come by and meet the champ. Little kids in the alleys and slums of Florida and New York, they can come and see me where they never could walk up on Patterson and Liston. Can't see them niggers when they come to town! So the white man see the power in this. He see that I'm getting away with the Army backing offa me . . . They see that we who're not flying the flag, not going in the Army, we get more respect . . . '

Clay picked up a back issue of *Muhammad Speaks*, the house organ of the Black Muslim movement, and pointed out several cartoons. One of them showed Uncle Sam whispering to the President: 'Hurry! Sign all those niggers into war so they won't be left behind us! . . . Let our own sons stay behind in colleges and universities! . . . No, we know we can't win!' In his hand Uncle Sam holds a paper titled: BILLS TO GIVE NEGROES DEATH IN THIS WAR. A young Negro man stands to one side, thinking, 'What shall I do or say?' and a tough-looking white man stands behind him, saying, 'G'wan, nigger, don't ask no questions!'

Another cartoon showed a Ku Klux Klansman starting to hang a Negro. Uncle Sam is grabbing the Klansman and saying, 'Hold it, stupid! We don't lynch niggers like that nowadays – we can draft them and get the same results.'

'Look at those cartoons,' the champion instructed. 'Look how bold our leader is. You know I gotta respect and obey a man as bold as that. If the government don't do nothing about it, then I gotta respect him.'

A few nights later, after Cassius had been firmly

entrenched in 1-A, a group of young men assembled in the living-room of Clay's house at 4610 N.W. 15th Court in Miami. 'We're here to see something big!' Clay advised me as I entered.

'Have a seat!' said Sam Saxon, one of the most enigmatic figures about Clay. 'Cap'n Sam' functions as a sergeant-at-arms in a Miami mosque of the Muslims, and Cassius himself refers to Sam as 'my bodyguard' (and at other times complains about newspapermen who describe Sam with the same word). Sam was one of Clay's earliest mentors in Black Muslimism, and later was promoted to the post of aide-de-training camp at a salary of $150 a week. Sam is a powerful Negro with blacksmith's arms, a light reddish-brown skin and brownish-amber eyes, a graceful man with an easy step and a shy smile that shows thin gold linings on his teeth. When he gets excited, his voice rises an octave and his words double in tempo, like a caricature Negro in an early film. But most of the time he is quiet and steady, a cafe-au-lait rock for Cassius to lean on, and although many old timers claim that Sam is one of the foremost white haters in the Muslim movement, he is capable of an occasional act of friendship such as borrowing your car or shaking your hand. 'Sometimes I get the feeling that Sam is putting me on, or putting the Muslims on, or putting somebody on,' said a friend. Perhaps this is because Saxon at least has a slight sense of humour, the rarest personality trait in the confraternity of the Black Muslims.

Sitting at the dining-room table that night was Rudolph Arnett Clay, whose father belatedly rechristened him Rudolph Valentino Clay and who has rechristened himself Rahman Ali. The younger brother of Cassius Clay, Rahman (pronounced 'Rock-mon') was writing a letter home to Chicago to his young wife, a task to which he gave intense concentration, except for occasional glances towards the television set that had been rolled into the stuffy living-dining area for the occasion. Rudolph is a very black, moustached man in his early twenties, and his appearance is as striking as that of the Rudolph Valentino for whom he was named. Another of Elijah Muhammad's true believers, he is also said to be an extreme hater of whites, although he manages to be civil to them. It is only after several talks with him that you begin to realise he is giving you the bare minimum of shrift with a friendly smile on his face.

Reggie, the driver and general helper, was also in the assemblage that warm evening in Miami, as were a few anonymous Negroes, the kind who wander off the street and are invited inside by Cassius because he admires their pigmentation. In the kitchen several Muslim 'sisters' pottered about in their severe white dresses, dis-assembling the evening meal. Back in a corner of the living-room, out of the way of the men, in the true Muslim tradition, sat an attractive Negro girl who was conspicuously not introduced to me. She remained silent throughout the evening. The entertainment before the house was the CBS news, and Sen. Wayne Morse was busily denouncing the U.S. role in Vietnam. 'See that?' said Cassius. 'All of them big men, they're saying we shouldn't go.'

The group watched silently as Sen. Russell Long asked Gen. Maxwell Taylor whether the United States was the international good guy or the international bad guy. Then the camera zoomed in on a newsman interviewing a GI at the front while shells exploded in the background. Cassius craned forward and said, 'Is that real shooting going on?' He was assured it was. The GI told his interviewer that the war was worthwhile 'and if I had anything to say about it I'd go home and spend a little time and come back again.' This brought a titter to the room.

Inmates of the Indiana Girls School rioted on the TV screen, moving Clay to shout, 'It's the end of time,' a favourite theme of himself, his real father, Cassius Clay, Sr, and his spiritual father, Elijah Muhammad. 'We're in the last days! The last days!' And suddenly a hush came over the room. Cassius Clay, the one and only Muhammad Ali, was on TV spitting out his anti-draft speech to newscaster Bob Halloran. 'Yes, sir, that was a *great* surprise to me. It was not me who said that I was classified 1-Y the last time . . . It was the government who said that I'm not able . . . Now in order to be 1-A, I do not remember being called nowhere to be reclassified as 1-A. These fellows got together and made the statement that I'm 1-A without knowing if I'm as good as I was the last time or better. Now they had thirty men to pick from in Louisville, Kentucky, and I'm also sure that there are at least thirty young men that they could have picked from. Instead, they picked out the heavyweight champion of the whole world. There's just one in my class. You have a lot of men in baseball they could have called. You have a lot of men in football they coulda called. You have a lotta men that they coulda called that are of school age and have taken the test that are 1-A. Now I was not 1-A the last time I was tested. All of a sudden they seem to be anxious to push me in the Army . . . And another thing I don't understand: *Why me?* A man who pays the salary of at least fifty thousand men in Vietnam, a man who the government gets six million dollars from a year from two fights, a man who can pay in two fights for three bumma planes—'

The interview came to an end in midsentence, and Cassius was on his feet in the room. 'That was a good one, wasn't it?' he asked nobody and everybody. 'Did Lyndon Johnson watch that? Is he watching this news or the other one?'

Saxon said, 'He's got 'em both on, one set on one and one on the other. Even if he missed it he'll get the tape of it.'

Cassius let that sink in, seemed to find it reasonable, and began to muse. 'Yes, sir, three bumma planes . . . That told 'em . . . That make it clear . . . '

When the newscast had ended, Clay announced: 'Elijah Muhammad been saying 1966 will be the end,' as though the news of the day had confirmed that the final year was at hand. 'Years ago he was saying the same thing. Thirty years ago.' Clay mused aloud about the President for a few seconds, but all I could make out clearly was, 'I wonder if he had me on.' *Stars in My Crown*, a homey movie about a Southern preacher, came to the screen, but it did not suit the champion's taste. 'C'mon,' he said brusquely to the mystery girl in the corner, 'we goin' fo' a walk.'

The next morning Clay had an early telephone call from Chicago. He was told that Chicago newspapers were on the street with stories that he would have to go in the Army and his scheduled fight with Ernie Terrell would be cancelled. The stories would kill the gate, Cassius was told, and he'd better correct them if he wanted to make any money out of the fight. Clay sat in his underwear next to the living-room phone and began burning up the long-distance wires. 'Hello, may I speak to Leo Fisher? Hello, Mr Fisher? This is Muhammad Ali, the world heavyweight champion. Ben Bentley [a promoter] was a talking to my lawyers about the fight. Something was out up there about the fight was off . . . Well, it's not. We're gonna appeal . . . Well, it's in the Islamic belief. We don't bear weapons. We don't fight in wars unless it's a war declared by Allah . . . Allah . . . Al*lah* . . . ALLAH! That's right. Anyone who understands the Holy Quran or the Islamic religion this is nothin' new or nothing . . . I see where the whites themselves are arguing, even in the White House they're on TV arguing every day. They're saying they're gonna get out and they don't like it. I see whites burning up their draft cards and they say it's a nasty war and we shouldn't be in it. That's what the senators and officials of the government themselves are saying. So our religion teaches me we don't participate in wars to take the lives of other humans . . . Well, I don't think they could be mad at me about what my religion teaches . . . Yeh, well, if their religion don't teach it I guess they go . . . '

After a few such calls he dialled a reporter (perhaps from the *Tribune*) who wanted to debate the subject, and Cassius went to the bedroom phone, shut the door and accepted the challenge. An occasional phrase was audible: 'Well, we'll make the appeal and the fight'll go on . . . We don't take up no weapons in no war unless it's a war declared by Allah himself . . . We are taught to defend ourselves if attacked . . . No, I don't know nothing about no Viet Congs . . . Well, the whites themselves have been demonstrating against the war. They're mad at the war . . . '

When the argument finally ended, and Cassius stomped back through the living-room in his battle raiment of undershirt, undershorts and socks, I said, 'Haven't you got enough to do?'

'Don't they keep me going?' he said, and laughed, pleased with his morning's work. Later, when his words on the draft were thrown back at him by the editorial writers and columnists, he claimed that they had 'taken my words as though I'm a politician,' and he issued broad suggestions to the effect that he was just a poor little ignorant fighter and he had been tricked and it was unfair to quote him on Vietnam and the draft and such weighty matters.

'As usual, you know me and my big mouth,' he said. 'It didn't get me in trouble in the past, but I spoke out on a few things that could be considered politics and I had no business doing it . . . I feel a lot better after calling, apologising to the [Athletic] commission and the boxing authorities who I put on a limb and caused 'em national embarrassment . . . I'm known for talking a lot.'

These alibis were not the real Cassius; they were dreamed up by people close to the money end of the fight, and he was mouthing the words as a personal favour to them. His explosive remarks to the press on the phone that morning had represented the most serious side of Cassius Clay, a fanatically religious side that only his closest friends understand. They were not surprised when Clay journeyed to the Illinois Athletic Commission and refused to recant. After all, Clay *is* a Black Muslim; his god *is* Allah; his hero *is* Elijah Poole, now known as Elijah Muhammad. Muhammad, 'the Messenger of Allah', served three years in prison during World War II for urging his flock not to go to war, and by his own reckoning nearly a hundred Black Muslims went to jail for taking his advice. Clay identifies closely with Elijah Muhammad, and takes orders from no one else. 'Cassius was searching for a father,' said a close relative, 'and Elijah Muhammad is it. If Elijah tell him, "Don't go to war, go to jail," he'll go to jail. That man have Cassius by the nose.'

Muhammad's book, *Message to the Blackman*, is studied by Cassius like a Bible (since his reading speed is below average, Clay often has passages read to him, and even enlisted me for the task once). The dominant theme of Muhammad's book is hatred of the whites. Beneath the fanciful tales about half-mile 'wheels' in the sky, '1500 bombing planes' preparing to wing down to earth and drop steel bombs into the earth on behalf of Allah, hidden in all the wild-eyed prognostication is a simple genocidal declaration of war against whites.

Cassius Clay has a blind and total belief in every word of *Message to the Blackman*, and thus he becomes a rare individual: a genuine, if misguided, conscientious objector. As a professional observer and friend of Clay pointed out: 'The government may say his religion is nutty as a fruitcake, but the government can't say it's not *his* religion. Now how the hell are you gonna send a kid like that to fight against people of colour, *his* people? How the hell are you gonna send him into battle alongside white Americans that he regards as the *real* enemy? That kid has a sincere, true, deep hatred of whites that goes all the way back to his childhood and the way his father brought him up. You meet the old man and you'll know exactly what I'm talking about. He set up an environment that made the Black Muslims or some other hate-white movement perfect for the kid. Some of these Black Muslims are just tough white-haters that find it convenient to belong, keeps 'em out of the hot sun, and a lot of 'em are making a buck off the religion, but Clay's really and truly hooked. The William Morris Agency told him he'd make a quarter of a million dollars a year in endorsements and advertising. About a week later he announced he was a Black Muslim and the William Morris deal was as dead as Kelsey's. He hasn't made a nickel off it since. Does that sound like somebody who's faking his religion?'

The idea of Cassius Clay's going to jail for draft-dodging would have brought a loud horselaugh not many years ago. 'I am going to be a clean and sparkling champion,' the young man from Louisville had said, and he was. No smoking. No drinking. No messing around. He was hailed as 'the new white hope' of boxing by at least one enthusiastic writer. His cheerful doggerel brought laughs from people who had no previous interest in boxing, and attendance climbed. Boxing had hit bottom in 1950, with total receipts down to less than $4 million. With Cassius carrying on, the sport took in $7.8 million in 1963, $18.1 million in 1964, another $8.4 in 1965. His antics benefited every division, and if he was a little wide in the mouth, who cared? It was all in a spirit of good humour; the public knew the kid was just building gates, and wasn't he good to his mother and father? His mother, Odessa Grady Clay, the very proto-type of the sweet, kindly Southern Negro mama, raved about him to the press: 'He use to say, "When I become champ I'm gonna buy you this and buy you that." And he'd sit and talk for hours at a time when he was twelve years old. He was gonna get me a house and furniture and a car and travel and anything else I wanted. *And he have done all those things!*'

Even allowing for the *ex post facto* myth-making that grows up around champions, Clay seems to have called the shot on a staggering number of achievements, including his Golden Gloves championship, his Olympic gold medal and his heavyweight championship of the world. His knockout predictions ('Powell must fall in three') were usually about stiffs, but it is not easy to flatten even a stiff in an appointed round, and the forecasts added zest to his appearances.

But as he got bigger and bigger, Clay began losing his sense of proportion. He seemed to skate right to the edge of mania in his pre-fight scenes. He lost track of the difference between buffoonery and nastiness, and the public began to sour on him. People close to him tried to make explanations and apologies. 'I'll never under-stand the resentment of his popping off,' said Angelo Dundee, the best trainer in the fight business. 'I remember when I was younger, hearing the people talk about, "Gee, Joe Louis is a great fighter, but he can't talk," and today you have a fellow who talks and fights and there's resentment. There's no figuring out the public. The public is a tough customer to be satisfied.'

So were the writers, especially after Clay began openly espousing the creed of Elijah Muhammad. 'Clay is likely to hurt the sport badly by his ideologisation of it,' William F. Buckley wrote. 'One can only hope that, to put it ineptly, someone will succeed in knocking some sense into Clay's head before he is done damaging the sport and the country which, however much he now disdains it, gave him the opportunity to hate it from a throne.' George Sullivan wrote: 'There was fun and amiability in Cassius Clay when he began his rise to national prominence. He was a popular good-looking youngster with a clean background – precisely what the stricken fight industry needed. Clay was regarded as the potential saviour of the sport, but some people feel he has been more of a hangman.'

When Sonny Liston remained affixed to his stool at the beginning of the seventh round in Miami Beach in 1964, Cassius Clay automatically became the best-known sports figure in the world. Europeans never heard of America's Koufax, and North Americans knew little about Brazil's Pele, and neither Americans nor Europeans knew of Red China's Chuang Tse-tung, but who didn't know who the heavyweight champion was? Clay mounted his pedestal and used all his power and glamour to become the most controversial figure in sport. Long before his unfortunate remarks about 'them Viet Congs', domestic and foreign reporters alike were lambasting him for lack of sportsmanship, for his tasteless bragga-docio, for his cruelty and his contempt of others. The 'clean and sparkling champion' was now being portrayed as a 'clean and sparkling bum', and more than a few people were taking nervous second glances at a remark made by Clay to Louisville sports-writer Dean Eagle. Full of himself and his glory, Cassius had said, 'I am the champion who will end all boxing.' Like most matters concerning Clay, the quote was paradoxical. His life is a symphony of paradoxes, and the biggest of all is that hundreds of thousands of words have been written about him, and yet his essential character, his attitudes, the fears and forces that drive him, remain unrecorded.

Part Two

'CASSIUS JR'S LIFE TO ME WAS AN UNUSUAL ONE FROM other Children, and he is still unusual today,' his mother, Odessa Grady Clay, observed in a hand-written biographical sketch of her son. Mrs Clay might have said that the whole family was unusual. For one thing, although they are Negroes they claim to be directly descended from Henry Clay, 'the great arbitrator', that troubled and perplexing figure in American history. 'Henry Clay was Cassius's great-great-grandfather, and that's no family legend,' said the fighter's aunt, Mrs Mary Clay Turner, the mathematics teacher. 'My mother and daddy told us about Henry Clay, and he left my grandfather a lot of money when he died.' On young Clay's maternal side there is another white man in the lineage: the champion's great-grandfather was an Irishman named Grady. Atop her bureau Odessa Grady Clay keeps a photograph of the Irishman's mulatto son, her father; the fading portrait shows a dignified-looking man with light skin, long hair and pale eyes. 'He looked exactly like a white man,' said Odessa, a pale golden colour herself.

The fact that he is at least partially white does not please black supremacist Cassius Clay, Jr. 'My white blood came from the slavemasters, from raping,' he explained to a racially mixed audience. 'The white blood harms us, it hurts us. When we was darker, we was stronger. We was purer.'

The original Cassius Marcellus Clay, Henry Clay's kinsman, was a historical figure in his own right. He lived in a plantation home, 'White Hall', near a little place called Foxtown in Madison County, Kentucky, and his fierce attitudes, especially against slavery, earned him the nickname, 'The Lion of White Hall'. 'He was opinionated, dogmatic and not very considerate of the opinions of others who disagreed with him,' according to Lexington attorney and historian William H. Townsend, a student of the Clay family tree. 'It is my understanding that the grandfather of the Negro boxer Cassius Marcellus Clay was a slave who belonged to the old lion and was liberated by him and that in gratitude he names his son Cassius Marcellus Clay, who, in turn, so named his son.'

The Lion of White Hall was one of the first Kentuckians to free his slaves and adopt a stance against slavery, backing up his position with a cannon which he once fired in his eighty-third year to scare off a posse out to get him. Once he was warned that he would be killed if he went to Stanford, Kentucky, to deliver a scheduled address against slavery. Clay walked down the court-room aisle in Stanford, stood behind the rostrum and said, 'For those who have respect for the laws of God, I have this argument.' He laid a Bible on the lectern. 'For those who believe in the laws of man, I have this argument,' he said, and placed a copy of the state constitution alongside. 'And for those who believe in neither the laws of God or of man, I have this argument,' he said, and laid two pistols, crossed with a bowie knife, in the middle of the lectern. The address went off smoothly.

'Yes, indeed,' said Cassius Marcellus Clay, Sr, father of the boxer and a man who likes to dip a toe in the main stream of history now and then, 'the original Cassius Marcellus Clay battled against slavery at all times. We proud of him. My own grandfather was brought up on

46

the old man's land, but he was never a slave. My grandfather was *with* the old man, but not in a slave capacity, no sir! Cassius Marcellus Clay took my grandfather with him at all times. And then my daddy was born. He turned out to be an ice, wood and coal man, my daddy. He was well off. There weren't no poor people in those days. I remember! Everybody made a pretty good living in those days. Every house in those days, when I was a boy, every house had so much food on the table that they didn't have time to put it in the icebox. They just threw the tablecloth over it. When I was a kid, they never took no food off the table. Had five or six different kind of meats on the table, ham, chicken, hot dogs . . . You'd come over to eat and they'd just uncover the table. My daddy had twelve kids, and now I'm the oldest living. Three dead now. I'll live to be a hundred and some years myself. Most of my relatives did.'

It is not too outlandish to suppose that the Clays of Louisville (Cassius Clay's father and mother and multitudes of uncles and aunts and his thirty-three cousins) might be waltzing to Lester Lanin or working on charity drives in Louisville's highest society if they were of another colour. Flair and energy and a degree of class emanate from almost all of them, down to the smallest children of the clan. There is hardly an adult Clay who does not hold at least two jobs and dabble in a variety of hobbies and outside interests like painting and Haydn and cabinet-making and geometric function theory. The Clays of Louisville are a *doing* family, alert and active, bright-eyed and intelligent, quick as chipmunks. But most of all they are a proud family. Pride is the common denominator of the meat-cutting Clay, the sign-painting Clay, the school-teaching Clay, the hair-cutting Clay and, almost to a fault, the prize-fighting Clay. 'There was a lot of trouble, bad trouble, between his father and mother,' one of Cassius Clay's early backers recalled, 'but Cassius

47

would bite his tongue before he'd mention it. He had too much pride. When he was fighting prelims on salary, he suddenly told Angelo Dundee that he had to have the money to go home right away, all the way back to Louisville from Miami. He'd gotten word his mother and father were gonna split up; and he was gonna go back and stop it. But Angelo was the only person he told, because Angelo wasn't gonna let him leave without knowing the reason. It's a very attractive quality in Cassius, not talking about his personal troubles. He'd talk about his dreams and ambitions but not his problems. Those were kept inside as a matter of family pride. They still are.'

Pride motivates the Clays of Louisville on many levels. It motivated some of them right through college, others to spend long hours in self-improvement courses at home, all of them to keep their houses a little cleaner, a little neater, than the next man's. Aunt Coretta Clay, a short, perky sparrow of a woman and a factor in Cassius' upbringing, said, 'There's some people that say coloured people are plain old lazy, they don't want anything, you put new houses for 'em on this street and in no time it's just gonna be all slummed up again, because they don't care. Well, you should have seen this house when we moved into it in 1940 – no trees, no paint, yard had nothing in it, no grass, no anything. The brick was just black with dirt, the mortar was old and rotten, and Cassius' grand-daddy was living then and he taught us, and we put on overalls after we finished work every day and we would scrape all the old mortar out and we got some tools and we tuckpointed the whole place. About seven of us at home then, and we did the whole thing in about six weeks. And then we plastered and papered the inside.'

While Coretta Clay spoke in the front room of her frame house in Louisville's West End, the matriarch of

48

the family, seventy-five-year-old Mrs Herman Clay busied herself at the end of a broom, sweeping up dust that did not appear evident to the naked eye. 'The Clays don't spend much time sitting around,' said Coretta. 'We're all active. I don't mean to be braggin'.' She offered some of her nutty fudge, one of the treats she makes ('Anything that'll make you fat!') and sells to neighbourhood kids. 'My nutty fudge won a blue ribbon at the Kentucky State Fair,' she said with typical Clay pride. 'Second premium, culinary, 1964.' She shifted to a note of regret. 'They said I would have won first prize but I put nuts on the inside *and* outside, and they were just supposed to be on the inside only.' Whenever a Clay fails to win first prize, you are going to hear an explanation.

Mrs Odessa Clay's biography of her son, the fighter, continued in ink on three-ring lined notebook paper: 'When a baby he would never sit down. When I would take him for a stroll in his stroller, he would always stand up and try to see everything. He tried to talk at a very early age. He tried so hard he learned to walk at ten months old. When he was one year Old he would love for some One to rock him to sleep, if not he wold sit in a Chair and keep bomping his head on the back of the Chair until he would go to sleep. He did not want you to dress him or undress him. He would aways crie. He wanted to feed himself when very young. At the age of two years old he always got up at 5 oclock in the morning and throw everything Out of the Dresser's draw and leave the things in the Middle of the floor. He loved to play in water. He loved to talks a lot and love to eat, loved to climb up on things. He would not play with his toyes. He would take all the Pots and pan Out of the Cabienet and beat on them. He Could beat on any thing and get rhythm. When a very small Child he walked upon his toes, By doing this he has Well developed Arch's, and that is why he is so fast on his feet.'

Odessa Grady Clay is not a Clay by birth, but she has absorbed some Clayness through the years. A kindly, endearing woman who is always fighting weight and losing, she discourses on her son Cassius as though she is talking about George Washington, and she can go for hours telling the kind of stories only a mother could love. 'Yes, sir, what I wrote there, it's perfectly true,' she said in her high, mellifluous voice, with some of her sentences ending, Southern-belle style, on a rising inflection. 'He walked way up on his toes, and he didn't quit that tippin' till he was five years old, and his grandfather said, "Odessa, he's marking you walking in high-heeled shoes!" He'd go *way* up on his toes? Oh, he was an unusual child all his life. So if people will read his early life they'll understand why he is like he is, I guess. He was queeeer? You never did see a child like him before. He was somethin' else! Whoo-EE!'

Odessa shook her head with the wonder of it all. 'Why, the first day of his life didn't start out right! They brought the babies around and I looked at the identification thing on his arm and I had somebody else's baby and Cassius was 'way down the ward with somebody else, the first day of his life! And every time they brought the babies out for feeding he would start crying and hollering and he would start all the babies on the ward crying and hollering. I'd just get so embarrassed! He did it every time. And then they brought that wrong baby again, and I said, "Nurse, this is not my baby! My baby's name Clay, this baby's name Brown," and she went down and got Cassius.

'He loved his bottle. You never saw a baby that loved the bottle like that, and later on he'd try to feed himself and he'd make the biggest mess. And he'd climb up in the sink to play in water. He loved water! He'd get into the washing machine and play in that water. And when we took him out he'd holler and kick and scream! And when he was a baby I would carry him around and everybody would say, "Well, there's another Joe Louis." '

'They would say, "You got a little Joe Louis there, sho' 'nuff, you got a little Joe Louis there," ' the father said. 'And him only a little baby! I was always excited about names, big important names. I wanted a Rudolph Valentino, a Cleopatra and a Ramona.'

'Yeh,' said Odessa. 'He wanted to name Cassius Jr "Rudolph" and I told him no.'

'I was crazy about Rudolph Valentino. He was so handsome.'

'But I thought Cassius was the most beautiful name for a man I ever heard,' said Mrs Clay. 'It's from the Romans, from Caesar's times.'

'Yeh, it's six thousand years old. That's what I'm trying to tell Cash about Muhammad, the name Muhammad. Cassius says his new name Muhammad is oldest and best. But his name can't be oldest and best because Caesar runs back three thousand years and Muhammad's name only runs back thirteen hundred and ninety years old. You gotta know history. Muhammad is the founder of the Islam religion. Thirteen hundred and ninety years ago. And the holy city was his home Mecca. That's just his home, it's not no holy place . . . I liked the name Cleopatra, too, because it's beautiful and it's Egyptian, too. I always liked Egyptian names. I like Egyptians, too. I like Indian names, you know. Like Chip-pee-wah, Ramona—'

'Little Cassius would always run as soon as he learned to get on his feet,' Odessa said, interrupting her husband's stream of consciousness. 'From the age of three or four till he got to be six or seven he'd run every place he went. He'd run ahead of us to church, run ahead of the buses, run everywhere!'

'Very energetic,' the father said.

'Yes, he was,' Mrs Clay hurried on. 'He was an active and noisy baby. He was always large for his age, and he soon outgrew his baby bed, he was *so* long, and he was so large we had to pay bus fare for him before it was time. I mean usually you don't have to pay till the child is five or six, but Cassius was only four when we started. And he loved to eat? And I would fix his school lunch and he'd eat it on the way to school. Every day he'd do that; so then I said I'd fix him, I'd give him lunch money instead. So he'd use the money to buy lunches from his friend Tuddie and eat Tuddie's lunch on the way to school.'

'Yeh, and he loved to talk, too,' Cassius Sr said. 'I'd come home and he'd have about fifty boys on the porch – this was when he's about eight years old – and he's talking to all of 'em, addressing them, and I'd say, "Why don't you go in the house and go to bed?" A whole neighbourhood of boys and he'd be doing all the talking. He'd always find something to talk about. That was in the old house at 3302 Grand Avenue. That's where Cassius spent most of his time when he was growing up.' The clapboard house Cassius Sr was referring to is no showplace: it is one storey high, a rectangular box sliced into four rooms, with a roof pitched at a slight angle to help the snows slide off, and a small backyard. The ornamental edging on the screen door was fashioned with a scroll saw by Cassius Sr, and the front steps were painted by him in red, white and blue after his son won a gold medal at the 1960 Olympics.

'Don't bother your head about that house,' Cassius Jr once said to *Sports Illustrated*'s Huston Horn, one of the first reporters to establish any rapport with the young fighter. 'One of these days they're liable to make it a national shrine. Only by that time I'll be long gone, man, living it up on the top of a hill in a house that cost me a hundred thousand dollars. You'll find me out by the swimming pool, and I'll be talking to a bunch of little boys sitting in a circle around my feet. "Boys," I'll say to them, "I was just a poor boxer once, as I reckon you already know. Only I was a very fine boxer, one of the finest that ever lived. And right there's how come I could move out of that little house down there on Grand Avenue and build this big one up here on the hill." '

'When he was young he always wanted to play with children that were older, and he wanted to be the boss,' Odessa Grady Clay continued. 'And he called his little brother Rudolph his baby? If I had to whip Rudolph, Cassius'd run and hit me and say, "Don't you whip my baby!" And he'd put his arms around Rudolph and walk him away and he'd say to Rudolph, "She better let you alone!" He was always a talker. He tried to talk *so* hard when he was a baby. He used to jabber so, you know? And people'd laugh and he'd shake his face and jabber so fast? I don't see how anybody could talk so fast, just like lightning. And he never sat still. He was in the bed with me at six months old and you know how babies stretch? And he had little muscle arms and he hit me in the mouth when he stretched and it loosened my front tooth and it affected my other front tooth and I had to have both of 'em pulled out. So I always say his first knock-out punch was in my mouth. He had so much strength he'd stand up in his baby bed and shake it and one morning he stood up and said to me, "Gee Gee", and that's what we all call him now. And later on in life he said he was trying to tell me "Gee Gee" for "Golden Gloves".

'I would make 'em take naps every day and one day he said to Rudy, "You know what, Rudy? We too big to be in here taking naps." And they never did take another one. And when they did little mischievous things I'd tell his father and he'd say, "Get in the bathroom!" Cassius Jr would always go in first and get his spanking and go right back out and do something else. He's something! I'm telling you! And love to eat? And get his spanking and go right out and do something else!' She paused to laugh. 'And one day his uncle took him out and a little boy was sitting in a chair and you know what Cassius did? He walked up to the little boy and knocked him out of the chair and he got in it and sat. He was a very unusual child.'

Cassius Sr re-entered the room brandishing some of his own paintings, but Mrs Clay talked doggedly on. 'You know when he was real small he wasn't afraid of but one thing, the onliest thing we would get out to make him behave himself. Do you remember what that was, Cassius?'

'These here paintings—' the father began, but Mrs Clay went on:

'He was afraid of nothing but a fur piece, like a collar on a coat, and if you told him you were gonna go get a fur piece you wouldn't have any trouble out of him and that was the onliest thing that worked that way on him. And he would sit down and be quiet and be scared to death. He was only about one years old when we first noticed this, and it lasted till he was about three or four years old. That was the onliest way we could get him to act right.' She laughed, and, pleased with her memories, she said contentedly, 'Oh, shoot!' Senior began passing some examples of his art work around, and Mrs Clay said:

'And he was always trying to work around the house and help me. The neighbours used to call him and Rudy "the gang-wreckin' crew" 'cause they'd go to visit his grandmother and run through every room in the house. They would run instead of walking. One day when Cassius was a little boy he chopped down our plum tree, of all the trees it had to be that one. Made his Daddy so mad! And he was always trying to frighten us. He would tie a string on to our bedroom curtain and run it to his room and pull it to make it move after we went to bed.'

'Yeh,' said the father. 'He'd do sumpin like that when I came home at night and I'd just say, "You can't scare me," and then he'd say, "Lookit, we scared him! We scared him!" and I'd say, "Look, you can't frighten me!" '

'And he'd put white sheets over his head and jump out at you in the dark,' Mrs Clay said. 'And he never was sick a day in his life except when he had measles and chicken pox at the same time. Ever hear of a child having measles and chicken pox at the same time?'

Cassius Clay, Jr is less likely to carry on about the minutiae of his childhood, being more concerned with the sublime events of his later years, but when he does start reminiscing his memories often tend to have a black thread of discomfort and pain running through them. 'We got into the house and the first thing I did was to run through the house and into the back yard,' he said one day, trying to dredge up his earliest memory, 'and there was an apple tree there and I climbed up and my mother told me to get down, and I pulled a green apple off of it and started eating it, and my mother told me, "You'll get the flux!" Some kinda disease you get. Some people die from it. Used to be a boy named Rudolph we used to be scared of. Every Derby Day we would look out the window and he would be parking people's cars. And there was another boy named Gunny, walked with his head in the air all the time. We afraid of him, too.'

Clay's childhood memories seem to run in a negative vein, with overtones of violence: boys who frightened him, foods that were poisonous, rock fights that were dangerous. But there was another violence that he never brings into the open: the violence in his home.

'I don't know whether you can understand it, being a white yourself,' said a very old friend of the Clays, 'but there's more apt to be a violent strain in a smart Negro family than there is in a dumb one. Dumb Negroes go their way like animals, just like dumb whites. Don't know whether the rain fallin' or the sun shinin'. Don't care. But the smart Negro could feel the pain of what was happenin' around him, and at the same time there wasn't a thing he could do about it, 'cept he could make it worse. So all this pain he kept bottled up inside, and he became quietly violent, and sometimes this passed on down to the kids. And every once in a while somebody'd shake the whole soda bottle and it'd explode right out in the open.'

There are hints that violence in the Clay line exploded in the case of the fighter's uncle, Everett, a mysterious figure whose demise appears to have come about in as many different ways as there are Clays to tell the story. Said Mary Clay Turner: 'Everett Clay. Everett the poet. He was very poetic, the most intelligent member of the family. He worked problems at Indiana University that no one else could, unsolvable problems.' How did he die? 'He just died. Everett just died. Very young, around thirty. Everett worried too much. He had a nervous stomach.'

Said Cassius Sr, Everett's brother: 'He didn't die, he got rid of hisself. The smartest one in the family, he died at twenty-eight, got rid of hisself. My daddy said Everett was too smart. He was a mathematician. He went to college and he led all the way through. But he was insanely jealous.'

A Louisville schoolteacher who lived a few doors from the elder Clays talked about the dead brother: 'Everett Clay was a wild man. He didn't care how big you were, he'd fight, and he wasn't big himself at all. Strange man.

Wore his hair long. He'd just *fly* into people.' According to the schoolteacher, Everett and his wife both died violently.

One of the first to realise that a tinge of violence may have touched the home life of young Cassius Clay was Patrolman Joe Martin of the Louisville Police Department, the boy's first boxing coach. 'It wasn't long before I knew the kid was scared to death of his father,' Martin recalled. 'I never got involved, but the fact I was a police officer must have bothered the old man. Years later, when Cassius was eighteen, we were all at Wilson Wyatt's office in Louisville to sign a contract for me to manage Cassius and train him. One of the lawyers took me aside and said, "I hate to tell you this, but old man Clay will not sign any contract with your name on it." I said, "Why, what's he got against me?" and the lawyer said, "Either it's because he thinks you've done something for his son that he couldn't do, or because you're a police officer." Later I read that the old man didn't like cops in general and me in particular. I knew why.'

The Clay family signed later with the Louisville Sponsoring Group, eleven wealthy citizens who took Cassius on almost as an act of civic pride. One of the original members of the group described an unpleasant note at the signing: 'There was Rudy, Cassius and Mrs Clay, all dolled up. We said, "Are you ready?"

'And she said, "Well, Cassius Sr isn't here." And we said we'd wait a few minutes and we waited and he didn't show. So we said we would have to go ahead without the father.

'And Mrs Clay said, "Oh, no, I couldn't do that."

' "Why not?"

' "Oh, he wants to be here."

' "Well, where is he?"

' "Well, I don't know."

'And Cassius Jr, who sometimes shows great maturity,

called us over to one side and said, "She's afraid of him. If we go on without him there might be trouble." This was our first inkling of the situation at home.'

The situation at home was volatile. Cassius Sr, a sign painter with minor artistic talents and a major taste for gin, engaged in periodic scuffles with his drinking companions, his wife and even his sons. 'He couldn't fight a lick,' a friend said about the senior Clay, 'but as soon as he'd have too many drinks, he'd take on anybody. And when he wasn't drinking, there wasn't a nicer guy in Louisville.'

More than once Odessa Clay had her husband brought into court for roughing her up. Cassius Sr was also picked up for reckless driving, disorderly conduct, assault and battery, always after he had been drinking. As another old friend put it, 'The father isn't a criminal or even an evil man. He's just a frustrated little guy who can't drink. He never served any time and he never will. Usually they put him under a security bond to keep the peace. If he'd lay off the gin, the police'd never hear from him again!'

Whatever fine distinctions could be made about the elder Clay's peccadilloes, Cassius Jr and Rudolph Arnett Clay grew up in an atmosphere of impending explosion (although each swore later, with hot Clay pride, that their childhoods had been happy and peaceful). Cassius Jr was not unmarked by the tension around him. A Louisville policeman remembered a call at the Clay's frame house on Grand Street:

'We got a report of either a cutting or a fight or something like that. We got there and Cassius had a cut on his thigh. His father wasn't there. Mrs Clay was raising—you know how women are. Cassius spoke up and he said, "My name is Cassius Clay and I'm a boxer under Joe Martin." And I said, "Well . . . ' I stuck my neck out. I should have turned a report into police headquarters but I failed to do it due to the fact I said to myself, "Well, there ain't gonna be no prosecution anyway," So I said to the mother, "Now look, take him to your own doctor or take him to the hospital, and if you want to, go up and take out a malicious cutting warrant." '

For the next three or four days, Patrolman Joe Martin, who collected coins for parking meters during the day and trained amateur boxers at night, wondered why his star pupil, Cassius Clay, failed to show at the gym. 'He was usually the first one to get there and the last to leave,' Martin said. 'Finally he came in and he was all patched up where he'd been cut. I asked him how he hurt himself, and he said he fell on a milk bottle.' All that remains of the incident in the police files is a mouldering entry in an old duty record book at headquarters: 'August 8, 1957— 10.32 p.m., Mrs Clay, cutting INV. [investigation] 3307 Grand. NA [no arrest].'

Before he stumbled on boxing, young Cassius appears to have spent some time running with street gangs. His father said, 'Whatever neighbourhood I'd move into, he would take up with the wrong gang. I had a hard time keeping him away from them gangs.'

'Oh, yes,' Cassius the champion said later with his usual wild hyperbole, 'I had the baddest street gang in Louisville. Who? Me! We carried pistols and shotguns and raced hot-rod cars, and we drinked and we got drunk and we went out having gang wars, shooting machine guns . . . '

In fact, the gang period was somewhat less dramatic than that, nor did it last long. Aside from the affair of the cutting, in which he was the innocent victim, Cassius was involved with the law but once, and then only because of childish stubbornness. He tells the story on himself: 'We were all at a skating rink one night, just before I was supposed to go to the Olympics, and somebody threw a rock and hit a passing car. Then he ran away. The police came and grabbed this fellow with me, and I knew he didn't throw the rock, and I said, "If you're gonna take him, take me, too." So they took us both. But when we got to the station they let me go home and him, too.' After Cassius won the gold medal at the Olympics, the arrest report disappeared from the Louisville police files. A Louisville newspaper reporter cherishes a photostatic copy of the report and tries to sell it to journalists studying Clay, but there have been no takers.

One night when Cassius was a skinny twelve-year-old, he ran into the man who was to change his life. Patrolman Joseph Elsby Martin, badge 474 on the Louisville Police Department, is one of those rough-cut gems who give the instant impression that they would have been successful in any career: atomic physics, horse-betting, or, in Joe Martin's case, a little of everything. He is bald, with an Alastair Sims-type baldness; his head is a high vaulted island of skin with fringes of white on both sides. He wears horn-rimmed glasses; his face is dominated by a large nose and his voice is soft and low except when he is angered. He lives in a comfortable home on the outskirts of Louisville, drives a Cadillac and vacations in Florida. Most people call him 'sergeant', on the theory that a man who has been on the force for twenty-five years ought at least to be a sergeant, but he is, in fact, still a patrolman, and for sufficient reason. 'I'm more interested in boxing than I am in police work,' Martin explained, 'and so I never took the examination for sergeant, for the simple reason that as a sergeant I would have had to give up my boxing job [director of boxing for the Louisville Recreation Department]. As a sergeant, I would have been put on swing shifts and one thing and another. I'm also a professional auctioneer and

I have a lot of sales, and it would have been a big loss in income to become a sergeant. 'Course, a lot of people call me "sergeant", and some call me "colonel", because the governor made me a Kentucky colonel, but I always stress on "patrolman".' Titles mean nothing to men like Joe Martin.

The young boys of Louisville used to come to the old Columbia gym in the centre of town to fight under Martin's direction, and when they learned their trade, they were put on a Saturday night television programme produced by the policeman. To make the TV appearance and especially a winning appearance, instantly elevated a boy in social standing around the various ghettos of the river city.

'I was down at the gym one night,' Joe Martin recalled, 'and there was something else going on in another part of the building, a display of merchandise that the Negro merchants put on once a year for their customers, like a home show. And one night this kid came downstairs from the show into the gym – we were in the basement – and he was crying. Somebody had stolen his new bicycle and he wanted to see the police and somebody had told him that I was downstairs. And he came down there to tell me and he was hotter'n a firecracker. He wanted to whip somebody and all that. I said, "Do you know how to fight?"

'He said, "No, but I'd fight anyway."

'And I said, "Well, why don't you come down here and start training?" I told him he better learn how to box before he goes out to whup anybody. So he started coming down, and he was a very faithful trainer, and that was the beginning of it with me and Cassius. And I can honestly say I enjoyed myself with him. I never heard him say a slang word, never heard him say a curse word, never heard him make any remarks toward any girls or about any girls.'

61

It took only a few months of Martin's training and Clay's natural ability to produce another fighter for the television show. 'He was twelve years old and he weighed eighty-nine pounds and I put fourteen-ounce gloves on him and put him in' against Ronny O'Keefe,' Martin said. 'That was his first television fight and he won a split. Three two-minute rounds, and those two boys really went at it! That was the beginning. Cassius had a hundred and six amateur fights altogether. I've seen figures where he had a hundred eighty-nine and two hundred and one and that's all false. All his amateur fights were with me and his last amateur fight was the Olympics and that was his hundred and sixth. Naturally, people are most interested in the fights he lost. Well, one of 'em was against Jimmy Ellis, who spars with Cassius now, and that night I shouldn't have let Cassius fight. He was sick. He insisted on going in so bad I finally let him. But Ellis couldn't have beat him if Cassius'd been feeling halfway decent. Cassius beat Ellis another time and he'd murder him now.

'One thing people don't realise: Cassius was a very fine loser. He always acted very graciously. I remember how gracious and nice he was after a southpaw named Amos Johnson beat him in the Pan-American Games up at Madison, Wisconsin. That was in the spring of 1959, and Cassius had won thirty-six straight, and he lost a split decision to this Johnson. Cassius always did have trouble fighting a southpaw and he always had trouble with anybody that could fight him inside, and Johnson could do both. If I was training a fighter to fight Cassius today, I'd tell him to get inside and stay there. That's where Floyd Patterson missed the boat.

'The only time Cassius was ever knocked out in the ring was when he was sixteen and fighting somebody much older named Green. The year before, when Cassius was fifteen, he'd had to lay out for a year because the doctor found a heart murmur. After a year the murmur went away and it's never been back. But Cassius was fighting this Green and getting shellacked pretty good in the second round. He wasn't hurt yet, but he was *gonna* get hurt, and I didn't want this, especially after the heart trouble. Green really rocked him in the second round and I didn't want to see Cassius hurt, so I threw in the towel. I tend to stop fights a little earlier than most guys, I guess. I hate to see my boys hurt. Cassius said he could've gone on, and I think he could've, but he'd have got knocked out eventually.

'Cassius really knew how to fight when he was in trouble. He never panicked or forgot what I'd taught him. When he'd get hit, he wouldn't get mad and wade in, the way some boys do. He'd take a good punch and then he'd go right back to boxing, box his way out of it, the way I taught him. In the finals of the Olympic trials in San Francisco, I remember he really got hit hard, knocked him clear across the ring and right up to my face. I saw he wasn't hurt, but he'd been hit hard. And whenever he'd get hit hard or made a mistake he'd always wink at me to show me he was all right. So there he was on his face in my corner, and I quick told him, "When you get up hook this guy in the belly and cross him with a right hand!" And he winked at me and got up and did exactly what I said and stopped the guy before the round was over. He would do what I told him. He always did.

'Only once did I ever see him knocked out, knocked cold, and that was in the gymnasium, working out with an amateur named Willy Moran. Moran was a good hitter. Later he turned pro as a welterweight, but he didn't make it because he wouldn't train. Anyway, he really flattened Cassius that day. Cassius had been talking to me about wanting a scooter, and when he regained consciousness, he said to me, "Mr Martin, which way was that scooter going that hit me?" The scooter was on his mind. That was the only time I ever saw him knocked cold. He was about sixteen then, and it didn't feeze him. He was back working out with Moran again the next day.'

Clay's lifelong fear of flying, a fear that remains with him, began during his relationship with Joe Martin, and for a time threatened to end his career almost before it had begun. 'That was the biggest problem,' Martin recalled, 'because as he got better and better he had to do a certain amount of flying, and it almost made him sick with fear. I think it all started on one of the first flights we made from Louisville to Chicago, and we ran into one of the worst storms you've ever seen. We hadn't been in the air over fifteen minutes when the stewardess came on and said, "Please fasten your safety belts, we're approaching Chicago." Well, I looked at my watch and I knew she was lying. Boy, it wasn't but a few seconds and we hit the damnedest storm you ever saw. I mean we was doing all kinds of flips and things were falling out on the floor, you know? And that plane started slipping down thataway and them motors just a-screaming and a-squalling. I really thought it was our last ride. I'd done made up my mind this was it. It was a little old two-motored plane. Finally the plane hit bottom and the pilot got it jerked up. We hit bottom so hard it pulled the screws right out of the floor where my seat was, and I had a black mark across my stomach where my seat-belt was. And I mean Cassius was praying and hollering! Oh, man, he was scared to death.

'Another time, when we were getting ready to leave San Francisco for Louisville, he suddenly said to me,"I ain't gonna ride a plane, I'm gonna catch a train." He wanted me to give him his ticket and I wouldn't do it. I said, "Nope, you either ride a plane or walk." I said, "I don't change my plans." I never would change my

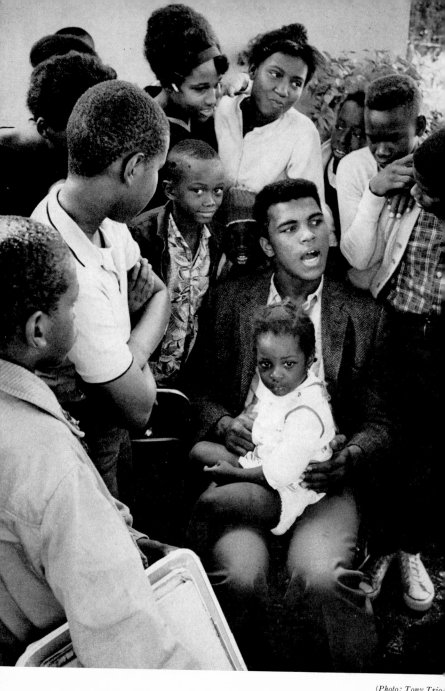

Cassius Clay in his Miami living-room

(Photo: Tony Trio

After driving his bus into a ditch in the Catskills

plans with any of those boys. When I told 'em sumpin, that was it. If I said it was raining outside, no use them looking. By God, it's raining! If you don't have complete control, you're in trouble. So I left him standing right there in Frisco, and he finally hocked his watch and got back to Louisville.

'When it came time for him to go to the Olympics in Rome, he came to me and asked me to arrange some way for him to get there on a ship. He didn't want to fly. But it was too late to get him on a boat. So I took him over to Central Park in Louisville and set him down and we must have talked for two hours. And I finally told him: "Now, look, Cassius, this is the way it is: I think you can be champion of the world but you have to win the Olympics." I said, "Now it all gets down to this: you can gamble your life if that's what you think a plane ride is, a gamble on your life, or you can stay here and forget about the heavyweight championship. If you think flying's so dangerous, why, you'll just have to take the gamble." So he finally decided to go.'

Hundreds of flights later, Clay is still deeply disturbed by flying, and avoids the airlines whenever possible. In the dead of winter, he will drive two thousand miles across the country rather than fly. Once he was flying from Las Vegas in a small commercial plane to referee a fight in Phoenix, Arizona. Soon after the take-off the pilot announced that there would be turbulence over Prescott, Arizona. Clay popped up in the front of the plane and asked where Prescott was. 'Between Kingman and Phoenix,' he was told.

'Good,' he said, 'I can get off at Kingman.'

'He said he wanted off the plane and he got off,' said a surprised stewardess, Donna Vans. 'I didn't realise who he was at first.'

'I really don't like to fly,' Clay admitted later. 'I say a prayer for a safe take-off and a prayer for a safe landing.

And I really feel out of place way up there at thirty-three thousand feet, cruising at six hundred miles an hour. You know what I mean? You're *really* out of your place. So most of the time I drive.'

Even when he is driving, flying is on Clay's mind. When a bus broke down on a long haul from Miami to Boston a few years ago, Cassius said to one of his companions: 'One thing about a bus when it break down. It don't fall no thirty thousand feet!'

At least one person close to him refuses to accompany Clay on any flights. 'He upsets me too much,' said Odessa Grady Clay. 'I remember one time when he was fighting in Nevada and he asked me to fly on the plane with him. On the first part of the flight, just the little stretch from Louisville to Chicago, he was scared to death. He asked me was I afraid? I said no. He said, "Wait till you get on this jet when we change planes at Chicago. They go much higher and faster and you'll be afraid then."

'So when we got on the other plane he said, "Mother, are you afraid yet?" and I said no and he said, "You just crazy." But it got on my nerves so bad to see him so afraid. I was already having ulcer trouble and I was so sick – my stomach hurt so bad. And he was just sitting up there scared to death; his eyes got real big and red and it got on my nerves something awful. He say, "If I get off this plane safe I'm going to go home by train." '

'Many's the time I thought his career wasn't ever gonna get started, and all because of that fear of flying,' said Joe Martin about his ex-protégé. 'He'd talk about it and worry about it. He's the type of boy that's fearful, anyway, and we'd be getting ready for a fight, a tough fight, and he'd be sitting around brooding about the aeroplane ride he had to take, instead of the fighter he had to face. But the thing you got to remember about Cassius is not that he's fearful, but that he's got the guts to overcome his fears. Nobody can help being afraid of

66

flying; if they are, they are, that's all. But to get on a plane and fly when you're shaking inside, that's something you got to admire. And I do admire Cassius. I spent six years with him, helping him, nursing him along, and I don't regret a second of it. Lately I've lost contact with him, since he turned professional, but he did donate a hundred-dollar seat for me at the second Liston fight in Maine. That's the only gesture he's made toward me since the Olympics, when I met him in New York when he came back from Rome. He sent me that hundred-dollar ticket out of a clear blue sky. A Louisville news-paperman called me one day and he said Cassius wanted to give me a ring-side seat for the fight, would I accept? They bought me a round-trip aeroplane ticket and paid all my meals and everything. It was very gracious of Cassius and the Louisville Sponsoring Group that handles him. I saw him at the fight, and he sat down and talked to me about thirty minutes, about some of my boxers and my son, Joe Jr, he's a good amateur boxer himself. Cassius didn't explain why he hadn't talked to me or contacted me for several years, and I didn't ask him, either.

'Then a little later Cassius Sr called me over to one side and he said, "Mr Martin, we made a mistake when we left you. We shoulda stayed with you." 'Course, the way the father is he might of seen me thirty seconds later and said the opposite. He's the character of all characters.'

Angelo Dundee, the trainer *par excellence*, was not expecting to run into any hotshot amateur boxers when he went to Louisville in 1958 with one of his fighters, Willie Pastrano, who later became light-heavyweight champion). 'Willie and I were laying around the Sheraton Hotel in Louisville a couple days before he was supposed to fight,' Angelo recalled, 'and we got a call from the lobby. "Hello, Mr Dundee?" This speaker pronounced it wrong, like D*un*dy. He says, "This is Cassius Clay, winner of the Pan-American games, winner of the Golden Gloves," etc. etc. etc. He describes everything he's ever done, and finally he says, "I want to talk to you." I held my hand over the mouthpiece and I said to Willie, "There's some sort of a nut downstairs that wants to talk to us. But he sounds like he might be a nice kid though." Willie says, "Why don't we send him up?" In the meantime this kid is chatting away on the phone telling me how he's gonna win the Olympics in 1960 and listing all the fights he'd won and people he'd beaten till my ear's about to fall off, and all this is only his way of introducing himself on the phone!

'So we invite him up and three hours later he's still there, talking. He brought his brother Rudolph with him and Rudy had some paintings with him – Rudy's a hell of a painter, I remember his work well. Cassius was asking questions about roadwork and how many times a day did Willie eat, how many rounds did he spar. He was hungry for information. I believe this is how he got the format for his training today. He got everybody's advice and condensed it into his own. And he made sure he learned only from the good ones.

'I got to know him better after that, on other trips to Louisville. He would work out and box with all the good fighters that came to town, and Louisville's always been a good fight town. He'd go to the gym and work out with both the opponents in the main go and then he'd tell 'em both they were gonna win. He'd tell each one things like, "You've got the perfect style to beat that guy." He wasn't being hypocritical; he was just trying to be nice to everybody. One day he had been working on the light and heavy bags and skipping rope for an hour before Willie and I got there, and then we let him work out with Willie. They boxed and Willie looked so bad I laid him off. This was three, four days before he was supposed to fight and I told Willie, "No more boxing, you looked awful!" And Willie said, "Ange, it ain't me. This kid is a good-looking fighter." Willie recognised his capabilities early.'

Soon after that, Cassius battled his fear of flying and took the plane to Rome, and the whole world learned what Willie Pastrano had already detected in the gym: that the young Negro from Louisville, pound for pound, was the class of amateur boxing. He won his early bouts easily and showed his Olympic team-mates the exuberant, good-natured side of him that was to distinguish him from other fighters in later years. 'He acted like he was running for office,' said a fellow Olympian. 'Everybody at the games exchanges pins from their countries, but Cassius made a career of it. Last time I counted, he was wearing forty-three pins, including one from the Soviets. And he'd run around the Olympic Village striking up conversations with anybody that'd listen to him. He was absolutely entranced by anything foreign. He was like a kid in fairyland.'

Already Clay's habit of predicting his victories was fully established in his personality, and he made no exception in his Olympic bouts. 'Why try to tell myself, "Maybe I'll win," ' Cassius told reporters, 'when I really think I will?' He came up against one Russian, Guennadii Shetkov, the 1956 Olympic middleweight champion and one of the favourites for the 1960 light-heavyweight gold medal, and Cassius talked as though he were preparing for a three-rounder back in Louisville on the TV programme. 'I saw the Russian fight, and I think I'll do the same against him as I did against the first guy,' Cassius explained jauntily. 'I'll wear him down in the first round by staying on him, then take him in the second. If I don't get him in the second, I certainly should get him in the third. If he goes that far, he'll be better than I think he is.' One was reminded of another Clay description of his fighting style: 'I like to hit a guy with two fast left jabs, a right cross and then a big left hook. If he's still standing after that – and if it ain't the referee that's holding him up – I runs.' He found no reason to run in the Olympic Games.

Even when he entered the ring for the finals, young Clay stayed loose, dancing and clowning in his corner in apparent disregard of the grandeur of the setting and the importance of the event. His attitude belied the fact that he had trained himself to a fine point for the fight, sometimes continuing his rope work and shadow-boxing long into the night, to the annoyance of his room-mates in the Olympic Village. He was eighteen years old; he had won forty-three straight fights, and he did not intend to let this one get away from him. Joe Martin had told him that the Olympic gold medal winner almost automatically becomes the Number Ten ranked fighter in his division as soon as he turns professional, and Cassius intended to become a pro as soon as the Olympics were over.

His opponent in the finals was Ziggy Pietrzykowski, a Pole who had won the bronze medal in the 1956 Olympics and had had 231 fights and fought southpaw, always a troublesome stance for Cassius to solve. This time it took him two rounds to figure out his opponent. Hands dangling at his sides, feet skipping around like an advanced Arthur Murray student, Cassius studied and studied, only occasionally deigning to throw a light lead. Several of the Pole's rights reached Clay, but he was always moving away when they landed. 'Man, I don't ever want to get hurt,' he had said before the fight, and to some at ringside it looked as though he was going to come out of the Olympic finals utterly unscathed and utterly devoid of the gold medal.

But at the beginning of round three, the crowd of

16,000 in Rome's Palazzo dello Sport realised instantly that the educational process had ended and the fight was about to start. Clay banged two heavy rights on the Pole's face and drew blood from nose and mouth. For the rest of the round, he battered Pietrzykowski from post to post, opening a cut over his eye and almost knocking him out on his feet. 'It was the bloodiest round of the Olympics,' wrote Martin Kane in *Sports Illustrated*. 'When the bell rang the Pole was all but defenceless, and had been so for at least the final minute.'

The day after the fight Cassius displayed more sophistication and political acumen than anyone had expected of him when a Russian newspaperman tried to exploit him with some carefully loaded questions. 'This Commie cat comes up,' Cassius recalled, 'and says, "Now how do you feel, Mr Clay, that even though you got a gold medal you still can't go back to the United States and eat with the white folks because you're a coloured boy?" I looked him up and down once or twice, and standing tall and proud, I said to him: "Tell your readers we've got qualified people working on that problem, and I'm not worried about the outcome. To me, the U.S.A. is still the best country in the world, counting yours. It may be hard to get something to eat sometimes, but anyhow I ain't fighting alligators and living in a mud hut."

'This cat said, "You really mean that?" and I said, "Man, of course I mean it. Who do you think I am?" Poor old Commie, he went dragging off without nothing to write the Russians!'

Small wonder that Cassius was hailed as a 'clean and sparkling champion' when he came back to Louisville. He wore the gold medal around his neck at all times, even when he was asleep (it was retired later, some of its silver underwear exposed where months of constant wear had rubbed off the gold). His sweet exuberance and naiveté charmed everyone. 'He acts like you would like a young American to act after receiving so much acclaim and so many honours,' said the mayor of Louisville after Cassius and Joe Martin were greeted by a police escort and a crowd of several thousand. 'If all young people could handle themselves as well as he does, we wouldn't have any juvenile problems. He's a swell kid.'

Soon there were various personages going about from podium to podium explaining how they had made Clay into an Olympic gold medal winner. Said Cassius: 'Man, it's like everything else. All the time somebody is telling me, "Cassius, you know *I'm* the one who made you." I know some guys in Louisville who used to give me a lift to the gym in their car when my motor scooter was broke down. Now they're trying to tell me *they* made me, and how not to forget them when I get rich. And my daddy, he tickles me. He says, "Don't listen to the others, boy; *I* made you." He says he made me because he fed me vegetable soup and steak when I was a baby, going without shoes, he says, to pay the food bill, and arguing with my mother who didn't want me eating them things so little. My daddy also says he made me because he saved me from working so I could box – I've never worked a day in my life – and he made me this and he made me that. Well, he's my father and he's the boss, and I have to pay attention. If I had a child who got rich and famous, I know I'd want to cash in too, like my daddy, and I guess more teenagers ought to realise what they owe their folks. But listen here. When you want to talk about who made me, you talk to me. Who made me is *me*.'

Whatever other explanations there were for Clay's relatively easy success at Rome, the major difference between him and his opponents was conditioning. To Cassius, it was not enough to have a splendid physique and the reflexes of a coiled adder. He worked like a

Versus Liston, Heavyweight Championship bout, Miami 1964

(*Photo: Tony Triolo*)

Victory over Liston, Miami 1964

coolie, from the age of twelve on, to sharpen himself into the best fighting machine of his era. When other boys were playing around with cigarettes and nude revelations and the other games of adolescence, Cassius was rising at 5 a.m. for roadwork, racing the bus to school, running around the track at lunchtime, returning to roadwork right after school and boxing in the gym at night. His self-denial was so extreme that it bordered on the unreasonable. *Nothing* interested him except boxing. 'From the age of twelve he just lived at that gym,' said his Aunt Coretta. Said another relative: 'Cassius was looking for a refuge, and he found it in boxing.' The champion's own version of his mad dash into boxing went as follows:

'Well, it's all I could really do. I saw there was no future in getting a high school education or even a college education. There was no future 'cause I knew too many that had 'em and were laying around on the corners. A boxer has something to do every day. Go to the gym, put on my gloves and box . . . There wasn't nothing to do in the streets. The kids'd throw rocks and stand under the streetlights all night, running in and out of the juke joints and smoking and slipping off and drinking, nothing to do. I tried it a little bit, used to try, wasn't nothing else to do till the boxing.'

Clay's single-mindedness about boxing, keeping in shape, putting temptation behind him, carried over to his early professional years, when the extent of his self-deprivation continued to baffle outside observers. Not that Clay was unaware of the strain to which he was subjecting himself. Nor did he fail to put in an occasional lukewarm complaint. One night a reporter found Cassius in a stifling hot hotel room, out of town for one of his early pro fights, going about his pre-bedtime activities by the dim light of an underpowered lamp. The hardest part of the training is the loneliness,' said Cassius. 'I just sit here like a little animal in a box at night. I can't go out on the street and mix with the folks out there 'cause they wouldn't be out there if they was up to any good. I can't do nothing except sit. If it weren't for Angelo, I'd go home. It's something to think about. Here I am, just nineteen, surrounded by showgirls, whisky and sissies, and nobody watching me. All this temptation and me trying to train to be a boxer. It's something to think about.

'But it takes a mind to do right. It's like I told myself when I was little. I said, "Cassius, you going to win the Olympics some day, and then you're going to buy yourself a Cadillac, and then you're going to be the world champ." Now I got the gold medal, and I got the car. I'd be plain silly to give in to temptation now.'

Prizefighting had always given Cassius the ingredients for his dreams, even as a young boy. Louisville's uninspiring West End ghetto did not provide the stuff that dreams are made on, but the rich world of boxing, with its Sugar Ray Robinsons and their lavender Cadillacs and its Rocky Grazianos with their books and movies, gave the boy all the material a questing mind could ask. 'Lunch hours and times like that I'd imagine I could hear my name announced as the champion of the world,' he said. 'One night I heard Rocky Marciano fighting on the radio, and all the excitement! "The heavyweight champion of the world!" "Marciano hit with a left!" "Marciano connects with a right!" "Now the champion of the world comes out!" And it sounded so big and powerful and exciting. Here I was a little Louisville boy riding around on a bicycle, no money, half hungry, hearing about this great man Marciano.

'And boxing made me feel like somebody different. The kids used to make fun of me: "He thinks he's gonna be a fighter. He ain't never gonna be nothing." But I always liked attention and publicity, and I used to race the school bus and beat it in twenty-eight blocks. Attracting attention, showmanship, I liked that the most. And pretty soon I was the popularist kid in high school. The other boys used to walk around with the school jackets on, and I'd walk with my jacket on, "National Golden Gloves Champion." That was a big thing, U.S. champion, and then I had "World Olympic Champion." I used to sit in school before I won the Golden Gloves and just draw the back of a jacket and write "National Golden Gloves Champ" on it, and then I would write "World Olympic Gold Medal Winner" on it, and then I would sign my autograph: "Cassius Clay, World Heavyweight Champion." I used to do all that, just wishing one day that I could do it for real.'

No one will ever know the exact extent to which young Clay's home situation steered him on the path toward the world championship (and beyond that, toward becoming the most despised and misunderstood sports figure alive). The immediate family's official version of the childhood of Cassius and his brother Rudolph is that all was bliss, and most of the other relatives are like Aunt Coretta, who intoned faithfully: 'People don't understand him, but we do, because we lived with him. His image to us is different from the public's. If they knew him they'd let up on him. They think he's arrogant and insubordinate. But he's a very nice boy.'

Aunt Mary Clay Turner, pugnacious, blunt and unpretentious, discussed the subject one evening at her small home on the outskirts of Louisville, her stockings comfortably rolled to just below the knee, sipping infrequently from a half-pint bottle wrapped in paper, sitting alongside a stack of books on point set topology and geometric function theory ('I'm taking a course in that mess right now,' she explained). In a bedroom, one son was practising the guitar and another was finishing an oil painting. Out on the front sidewalk young Roger, 'my scientist', examined the craters of the moon through a 60 mm. 240-power refracting telescope, while the remaining three children were loudly involved in television, to their mother's annoyance.

'Here,' she said, offering glasses and bourbon all around. 'Pour yo' own trouble. I have it every Friday night to relax after teaching school all week.' She talked about Cassius in admiring terms. 'He said he was gonna do all these different things and he did them. That's why we were *so* proud of him.' What had happened to turn him into such a sour public figure? Aunt Mary hesitated. 'There are certain things . . . A story stops some place, you know? If I told the whole story they'd all give me the bad eye when I go to school. But I know why he acts the way he does. I don't blame him. I'm just speaking of a number of events, not just one thing. *Numerous* events. Our family has it figured, what happened to him. The papa has it figured, too. *He* knows. But the papa never would say anything. If Cassius tells you he's the way he is because he was kicked around by white people, he's just trying to give you an answer, that's all. If that boy got it into his heart to give you the real answer, you'd almost die. Deep down he doesn't believe in the Muslims, he's not that way. He doesn't hate whites. He receives whites very nicely. He's never sent *me* a hundred-dollar ticket to a fight, but I'll bet he's sent his friend Henry Sadlo one. What colour's Sadlo? White, right? He sent Joe Martin one, and he's white. And he paid Henry Sadlo's fare to a fight. His mama wanted me to go to a fight with her and he wouldn't let me.'

Aunt Mary made it clear that she was not excusing anybody or setting up any cheap alibis. '*All* kids are affected by what happens with their parents,' she said, 'but some children try to rise above it. I work with those kind of kids whose parents knock each other down, drag each other out. The kid comes to school with a big old

76

knot on his arm or he comes with a big welt on his head, and he makes up his mind he's gonna overcome it. And that means you have to be strong. *If you're weak, stay home!* I remember the day I told my mother I wanted to go to college. "Well, if you go, you'll go over my dead body, 'cause Everett went and he didn't do nothing with the education." I said, "Well, just give me ten dollars and I'll get the rest." I put an ad in the paper asking for work and I worked clear through school. You have to be strong in your own way.' Aunt Mary paused. 'Here,' she said. 'You want to cut it with water?'

'Y'all like to have a little gin highball while we talk?' Odessa Grady Clay asked. 'Well, I'll just sit here with you and have one. I'm on a diet.' She sat on the sofa in the red-brick bungalow that her son bought in an all-Negro section of suburban Louisville called Mont Clair Villa, a sort of sepia Levittown laid out like a Monopoly board on flat, dreary farmland. The snow was general all over Kentucky, temporarily mantling the two Cadillacs in the driveway, 'his' and 'hers', hand-me-downs from Cassius Jr. If Mrs Clay was aware of the racial cliché expressed by two big Cadillacs sitting in the driveway of a little $17,000 home in a Negro neighbourhood, she did not let on. The radio was loud and unremitting at its permanent spot on the dial, WAKY, Louisville; the background music consisted of an ear-splitting outfit called Sam the Sham and the Pharaohs, whose gal was red-hot and hit the spot, or something to that effect. Mrs Clay did not seem to notice the din; it was a constant, and the Clays adjusted their hearing and speech to it. She sat calmly, a fleshy, coffee-skinned lady with big freckles, conspicuous rouge and lipstick, starkly pencilled eyebrows, lightly pomaded black hair; she was wearing a pair of velvety pedal pushers and several layers of light

77

material around her shoulders, like a Hindu princess. When she laughed, which was often, in rich and contagious tones, one could see the gold edgings around the two front teeth that were replacements for the ones Cassius damaged when he was a baby.

Her husband, Cassius Marcellus Clay, Sr, a miniature volcano of a man, strode into the room bearing documents. 'Here's a picture of me when I was younger!' he said in his staccato, out-of-breath manner, words tumbling over one another, making him difficult to understand. 'Don't I look like an Arabian? All my features are Arabian. I got an Arabian book here. My sister gave me this book twenty years ago. I study it to find out what's going on in the world. Here, looka this!' A picture of a flock of sheep was captioned: 'These sheep follow their leader blindly. They do not know where they are going. They cannot choose a way for themselves.'

'That's Cassius and all of Elijah Muhammad's followers right there!' the father said excitedly, gulping for breath. 'Read it again! Ain't that Muhammad's followers?' He laughed uproariously.

Mrs Clay said, 'When their father showed that to the boys they got so mad? But then they have a good answer.'

'Yeh,' Cassius Sr said. 'They sound like a broken record. They say the white man wrote that.' The Clays laughed together.

Cassius Clay, Sr, is a quicksilvery little man, the leading player on any stage he visits, a man who does not mind telling you that he is the hippest, the wisest and the coolest. 'I always wondered where the champion got his quick ad lib,' trainer Angelo Dundee once said, 'and then I ran into his father on the street and I knew. His father looked like a young jitterbug himself, ageless, in the same shape as a young man, and just as sharp.' Cassius Sr is several shades darker than his son, and almost as handsome in a basic sort of way. Unlike Cassius Jr, the father has a flat Negroid nose and wears a slightly lopsided moustache. His face is well chiselled, his eyes deep-set and black, his short dark hair receding only slightly and hardly greying despite his fifty-four years. But his most memorable characteristic is his manner of speech. He huffs and snorts and says 'Ummmmmmmm' loudly; his arguments take form as loud outbursts accompanied by agitated wavings of the arms; he stutters and swallows and backs up and repeats and runs into the bathroom to spit. He has no speech defect except an uncontrollable urge *to be heard right now!* But just when you become convinced that he is about to lose all control of himself, Cassius Sr will break into a laugh, a big old rapscallion laugh, and make you wonder which parts of his diatribe are real and which parts are not. There is a child-like quality to the man, and something of the Bohemian artist laughing at reality. Much of his life has been spent on the brink of make-believe, but no one knows for sure whether he is kidding himself or kidding the people watching him.

'Old Cassius has claimed to be a sheik, a Mexican, a Hindu, always something way out,' said an old friend. 'At one time he wore a great big hat with tassels on it and a shawl across his shoulder. He was being a sheik then. That's what he was when Rudy was born, that's where the name came from. He never was a Moslem, but he did say he was an Arab, and an Indian from India or something. At noon he used to get down off his painting ladder and in his little box he had a carpet and he'd put this carpet down and bow to the east and then bow to the west. When he was in his Mexican period he'd even lie down and pretend he was taking his siesta. Later on he was a troubador, singing in the streets. People'd be trying to sleep, one, two in the morning. They'd say, "Here comes Cassius!" He used to sing at night-clubs if they'd let him, or in the streets if they wouldn't. Love to sing!'

Striding about his living-room, mixing and re-mixing frequent infusions of gin and Squirt, Cassius Sr looked more like a twentieth-century jazz musician. Lean and loose and light on his feet, the type of man who wears clothes well, he had on black slacks that hugged tight to his body, and a knitted sports shirt in broad vertical stripes of red, grey and black. The only discordant note was in his shoes: long, thin black shoes of a sort that one never sees on a white man, smooth shoes with a gentle curve, six rows of laces, a high shine, the kind of shoes one associates with Bojangles, Stepin Fetchit, railway porters.

'I hate those kid singers,' the father said, apropos of the radio. 'Now that guy that sings "Crying Time", what's his name? Ray Charles. He's something else! Dean Martin's *my* singer, man!' Then, with no trace of a warning, Cassius Sr skipped on-stage, front and centre, and began to sing: 'I'm looking for an angel . . . to croon my love songs to . . . ' His voice was warm and on key, with an over-sized vibrato and a slight husky quality and trace elements of other Negro voices: Nat Cole, Joe Williams, Billy Eckstine, Herb Jeffries. ' . . . But until the day that one comes along, I'll sing my song to you.' He got the words mixed up, backed off and tried again, giggling once with nervousness but deadly serious underneath, and finished on a triumphant high note to polite applause. 'Wait-a-minute-wait-a-minute-wait-a-minute!' He said three 'wait-a-minutes' in about a half second, and launched into a whistling reprise full of double stops, glissandi and grace notes.

When he came up for air, Cassius Sr asked if he could sing one more, 'one of my good ones', and without waiting for an answer he began. 'We Can't Go On This Way', taking special pains with the release, 'Hiding behind the mask of laughter . . . ' which he pronounced 'the mosk of loffter'. When he had finished, he turned excitedly to his audience. 'Never heard that before, did you? Ummmm? Ummmmmmmmm? Ummmmmmmmm! I'm keeping that song, yes, sir! That song goes back . . .' deep breath . . . 'a long ways . . .' Deep breath . . . 'Now let's try "Ramona".' At the end of the opening phrase, Mrs Clay said loudly, 'Have some coffee. The pot's warm.'

Cassius Sr gave her a look and went on: ' . . . Ramona, we'll meet beside the waterfall.' He was caressing each syllable now, bedazzled by the beauty of his own tones, the exactness of his own pronunciation. ' . . . I'll always re-mem-bair, the rambling rose you wore in your hairrrrrrr.' Then he opened up on an old Glenn Miller hit, 'Careless', but Mrs Clay began chatting merrily away about her son the prizefighter. 'Wait a minute!' Cassius Sr said. 'Let me break in, make an entrance!' He ducked into the kitchen, came running out in the mincy style affected by some night-club singers, extended his arms like Bobby Breen and began: 'Careless, now that you've got me loving you.' At the end he was breathing hard, clearing his throat and gulping and still trying to talk. 'Yes, I-was-a-sign painter!' he said rapidly. 'People-used-to-hear-me-sing-and-they'd-say' – deep breath – ' "Man-you-missed-your-calling! You-a-singer!" '

He was asked if Cassius Jr could sing.

'Cassius? My brother? I mean, my son? If he kept on, he could sing. All of them, when they start out they're nothing. Nat King Cole was nothing when he started out. And Dean Martin was nothing. Frank Sinatra was sickening. Frank Sinatra was *sickening!* Cassius's a good singer, but none of 'em got a voice like I got. But he's a good singer. Not as good as me, but he's good. His voice got to be cultivated. Rudy can sing. But none of 'em got a voice like I got. They can't whistle like I can. 'Cause I can whistle! "Indian Love Call", all them kind of songs, you know?'

The conversation veered from music to religion, and Senior stated his personal position without prompting: 'I'm a Methodist and I'll be a Methodist till the day I die! 'Cause my mother took me there and had me christened when I was six months old. And anything my mother did I know was right because I was born from my mother and if it wasn't for my mother I wouldn't be here. And I wouldn't change my name for nobody. Because my mother named me Cassius Clay.' His fast delivery grew faster, and he jumped to his feet. 'My mother brought me up and she's the cause of me being where I'm at today. My mother had a talent and I was it, and it's been brought out to the world and my sons! My mother wanted me to be a musician. She did everything in the world to make me a musician.' Without breaking stride, he said suddenly: 'Eh, now wait now, what about some money before we start talking about Cassius here? I'm gonna give you a heck of a story, starting off now. There's got to be some money. This story's gonna be worth millions, because it's Cassius Clay's life. The greatest fighter ever produced. The greatest contract ever written was written by Cassius Clay, Sr and it was handled in Louisville by honest men, rich men . . . So where's the money? I'm a money man. I'm crazy for money! I need money!'

Both the senior Clays share with their prizefighting son the conviction that the mere mention of his name is worth barrels of cash. They are certain that a book about him would be an instant best-seller, articles about him would automatically double any magazine's circulation, and food products that used his name would drive competition off the market over-night. 'We're gonna make a lot of money in advertising,' the father said. 'You know, endorsements? So we don't want to spoil that by giving away the names of foods he ate, things he drank. So we'll just say in his life story, "I believe he was a born champion, waiting to be cultivated. And one great cultivation was Pet milk—" '

'No, no,' Mrs Clay interrupted. 'We won't name the milk, we'll just say "the milk his mother gave him." And we'll say, "His favourite baby food, he loved and ate so much of it." But we ain't gonna give the name of it. Then we can sell advertisements to them later.'

'Yeh,' Cassius Sr said. 'I'll call up three baby foods but in the meantime we'll leave the name wide open.'

The two parents fell to exchanging reminiscences about their son in the staccato style of the Clay family:

He: He always was the most energetic child I ever seen.

She: He sure was. I'll tell you, you never seen a child like him before.

He: Funny now, wasn't it?

She: He was *too* much.

He: Always goin'.

She: I'd get so tired. I had two cousins and I'd say, 'You all take him down the street in the stroller,' and in about five minutes they'd come back and say, 'Here, take this boy, he just won't sit down and do right.'

He: Tell 'em about the gang-wreckin' crew.

She: Yeh, that's what they called 'em.

He: They ate so much. I went to the grocer to get vegetables to make soup, and he said, 'What you gonna make that soup in, a tub?'

She: And he used to want you to sing him to sleep, and if you didn't sing him to sleep he'd just rock and bump his head? You remember, Cassius?

He: UmHmmmm. Sho' would, wouldn't he?

She: Like it didn't hurt his head at all.

He: He'd bump his head.

She: Bump his head real hard.

He: Real hard.

She: Settin' in the chair.

He: How'd he do that? That'd give me a headache!

But it is not possible for Cassius Clay, Sr, to keep up an interest for any length of time on subjects other than Cassius Clay, Sr, and soon he was taking the visitors on a guided tour of the basement room he had refinished. It was a sprawling room, panelled in plywood and dominated by four glassed-in pillars throwing a dull ocherous light from their innards, a type of illumination seen in some taverns and a few night-clubs in Tijuana. On the walls he had affixed wooden musical notes and a G-clef sign, a handful of wooden playing cards and two wooden pairs of dice with the spots placed incorrectly. In a corner was a dusty twenty-seven-inch television set, a stereo radio, another television set and a phonograph, gifts from Cassius Jr.

In another corner, lined up against the wall, were several of the father's oil paintings: rural scenes of a flashy quality, one showing metallic red glows in the clouds and purplish snow over the land, another of a red barn, an old carriage waiting outside and a carriage wheel propped against the wall. While his visitors watched in puzzlement, Cassius Sr plugged in two motorised spotlights with revolving coloured lenses – orange, red, blue, green – and allowed the artificial colour to splash over his paintings. 'Sumpin', isn't it?' he said proudly. 'Now it's sunset, about five-thirty in the evening.' The disc turned. 'Now it's night-time. Now watch! The sun's coming up. Wait a minute now. It's the middle of the day!' He said he liked to come into the basement, pull up a chair and study the effects of the colour wheel on his paintings. 'When I put on my exhibition down-town, I'm gonna use these lights,' he said. ' 'Course, I still have some more paintings to do for my one-man show. I'm gonna paint the Mona Lisa, bring it out a little, highlight it, make her stand out . . . ' It was all reminiscent of Dali's 'Mona Lisa with Moustache', with op art overtones.

84

'Some of my best work can't be shown,' the father went on proudly. 'My murals are in every new church in Louisville. They're beautiful, aren't they, Peaches?' Mrs Clay said they were beautiful. 'Now in Cunningham's church I have five scenes,' he rushed on. 'The Conception, the Birth, the Baptism, the Crucifixion and Jesus Knocks at Your Door. That's your heart, the door is your heart.'

Back upstairs, Mrs Clay tried to steer the conversation to the subject of her son. 'Do you remember how he used to chase chickens?' she said.

'He used to chase *my* chickens,' the father said. 'I used to have five hundred chickens. You know what I can do? I can raise ninety chickens out of a hundred. That's sumpin', ain't it? A farmer asked me to explain how I did that. I said, "That's *my* secret!" ' He sat straight up, a little peacock, and accepted the group's admiration modestly. But a few minutes later he became enraged, momentarily, when someone mentioned that Cassius Jr was talking about writing an autobiography under his new Muslim name, Muhammad Ali. 'I understand the whole thing!' the father said, rushing about the room snorting and sniffing angrily. 'I dig now! *I dig now!* What they're trying to do is erase that name out. *Cassius Clay*. That name's gonna be pushed! That name shall not die! Now look! You and I're gonna write a book, too. It's gonna be on Cassius Clay, Jr. It'll be called . . . ' His voice lowered to a dramatic whisper, '*A Boxer Was Born*'.

'Now remember this,' he went on, back in high gear. 'In anything you write about me, do not mention Elijah Muhammad's name. You know why? Every knock is a boost. He wants advertisements. I'm not advertising Muhammad. If Cassius tells you anything about Muhammad, just take it in your head but don't write it! Don't help Muhammad in no kind of way. It'll make him mad if you don't write about him!'

'Little Cassius was in Louisville for Christmas,' Mrs

Clay said at her earliest opportunity to break in. 'He stayed at the Sheraton downtown. Cassius and Rudolph have a nice room here, but he stayed downtown. Cassius's in town right now. With Joe Louis. He came out to visit us, but he only stayed twenty-five minutes, kept a cab waiting outside in the driveway. He hasn't been back since. He's been told to stay away from his father because of the religious thing, and I imagine they've told him to stay away from me, too. Muslims don't like me because I'm too fair-complected.'

'They keep him away from me,' the father said. 'They know I could bring him right back to the church. They tell him he can't stay around his parents. They know I know too much about the Bible. That's why nothing the whites ever did could annoy me. Because I knew the day would come. See, I know the Bible, every day I read the Bible. The time hasn't come yet, the Bible tells you. Ummmmmmmm? But now God is stepping into the picture. It's time now. It's like the days of the Pharaoh. God wanted Pharaoh to do the bad things that he did. God wanted it done for a purpose. God can soften or harden a heart.' A Southern Railroad freight train rattled by behind the house and blew long and loud for a crossing, and when the noise subsided Senior was still rambling on. 'God was talking to St John at the time, and St John said, "How will we know when it's judgment time?" . . . and God said, "You'll tell winter from summer by the leaves on the trees," and that's the way it is now. Sometimes you have cold days in the summer-time and warm days in the winter-time, and God says man'll be loving man, and there's that, and God says there'll be thunder and droughts and earthquakes, more than ever, and there'll be more tearing down and destroying and building up, more than ever. Am I right? Ummmmmmmm. You're in the last days! The time is now! The last days! 'Course, He's not gonna destroy the planet. See, I read the Bible. All this stuff stays here. And God will rise the Christians. The people like Muhammad's people, they will not be in the first resurrection. Father Divine and Daddy Grace and all them will be with the non-Christian people.'

Mrs Clay started to laugh. 'Father Divine, Daddy Grace,' she repeated, and the very mention of their names convulsed her. The Clay's Christianity is an absolute, admitting of no possibility of error, and they have no time for sects or other religious points of view. Senior is fond of saying 'according to the Scriptures', and when you point out that he is quoting from his own religion's scriptures, that other people have holy writ of their own, he goes into a long argument that Jesus was sent to earth to eliminate the differences between religions and that all the others are wrong. If you persist in discussing other religions as though they were not entirely evil, Cassius Sr will say, not unkindly, 'Don't talk that Muslim stuff to me!' and cut off the conversation. He is as dogmatic about his religion as the most faithful Southern Baptist.

The phone rang, and Senior took the call. 'Hello?' he said, and, 'Just a minute.' He ran into the living-room excitedly and told Odessa *sotto voce*, 'It's Cassius!' She took the phone and spoke to her son with consummate tenderness, addressing him softly as 'Baby', while the father whispered to his guests, 'That's Cassius now.' Odessa hung up and Senior asked what their son had said. 'He's on his way to visit Coretta,' she said. 'They're making hamburgers. He says he's very happy, very happy.'

'He'll get away from them eventually,' the father said.

'Yeh, he's doing better all the time,' Mrs Clay said.

'He'll get away. A man can't stay on the wrong road too long, am I right?'

He poured drinks all around and began quoting loudly,

87

'Drink and be merry for tomorrow we all die,' rolling his r's and affecting an English accent. 'Who know what tomorrow will bring? It may bring rain, death . . . ' Dramatic pause. 'Or happiness. As we share this last drink, we share this last drink in blood. Let's share it together. I came not this time to praise thee, but this time to conquer thee.' Patiently he explained, 'That was Brutus, come to Caesar. He was Caesar's best friend, you know? Caesar was such a great leader, and masculine, you know? So they always come to praise him, and when Caesar took Cleopatra they went against him.' The father acknowledged that he had quit school in the ninth grade, but pointed out that 'environment is education.'

Then, his hands trembling with excitement and his words spilling out faster than ever, he told about his project for the future: a combined factory, restaurant and whatnot shop, all incorporated under the name 'Clay's Enterprises'. 'I want to do something like that so I can just be the supervisor, and I'll be helping my people a lot,' he said. 'They need jobs. A place with a name like that. "Clay's Enterprises", it's got to go over big. I'm cashing in on that name, see? Cassius Clay! Since Cassius is dropping it, he don't want it, I'll cash in on it. Since he done up and dropped it, that's his funeral. He's trying to kill that name, see? But he said he's gonna buy me some land to retire on. And I'm gonna build on it! When he comes back he's gonna see a big concrete building: "Clay's Enterprises". He's trying to rub that name out and I'm gonna make it strong! You dig? Don't forget, I'm the original Cassius Clay. He's just a branch!

'We'll have "Clay's Kitchens", right out there in the country, won't have so much overhead, have the factory right on the farm. Peaches and I will supervise, and I'll make the chili and the creole lunch. Peaches'll make home-made cakes and pies.'

Said Mrs Clay: 'He talks about it all the time.'

With a Muslim 'sister'

'That man, Liston!'

'I'm also gonna manufacture things for Clay's Whatnot Shops. I'm not gonna do all this myself; I'll have an assembly line. I got enough in my family to employ, I got twenty-five or thirty nephews to employ. Coretta's a wonderful cook, she's in business for herself, but I'm gonna get her out there. And I can cook. I'm one of the best. When I start Clay's Kitchens I'm gonna feature a creole dish and chili. And we're gonna have a new home, too. On four acres in Indiana. I have the plans drawn up already. Place'll be about two hundred feet back off the road. I love the country, man! I don't like no towns. When I was a kid, I always told my daddy – he was a ice, coal and wood man – I always told my daddy, "Let's go to the country".'

And now everyone was invited into Cassius Sr's white Cadillac convertible, vintage 1961, for a guided tour of his sign-painting accomplishments about Louisville. The car was cold, and a rasping noise came from under the hood while the broken speedometer needle spun wildly. The heater was out of order, the cigarette lighter was defunct and the horn honked whenever Senior made a turn. Used cigarettes littered the car and when the father finished another one, he ground it out on the edge of the glove compartment and stuffed it in a crack in the dash. He was singing 'This Is a Lovely Way to Spend an Evening', and he was garnished with a red hat, red plaid sport jacket, ankle boots of soft black leather and a black-and-white hound's-tooth check car coat. As we drove toward town, he pointed at houses: 'I'd buy that one if it was two hundred feet back off the road,' he would say, and, 'Look at that place, right on the highway, all them exhaust fumes and factory dust.'

He cleared his throat and treated his captive audience to a heavily stylized rendering of 'St James Infirmary Blues', leaning heavily on the Hot Lips Page version, and tacked on a snappy whistle reprise. 'We been in the blueblood neighbourhood long enough,' he said. 'Now we heading back to the po' people. There's sho' 'nuff po' people here!'

He stopped abruptly at a red light. 'Don't want no traffic tickets, don't want to have to bust no cop in the mouth!' He laughed. 'I'm the guy that always want to bust the cop in the mouth!' More laughter at himself. '—And he's the one with the two guns and the stick, and *I* want to bust *him!* Had an older brother did that to two cops, took away their guns and sticks and beat 'em up . . .'

He made a quick turn across two lanes of oncoming traffic as the light was changing, and Odessa said from the back seat, 'You can't cut those cars off like that, Cassius! You'll get us hit that way!'

'You *gotta* cut 'em off,' the father said. 'This is the atomic age, Peaches! Judgment Day 'round the bend! You back in another age.' He whispered, 'When she tries to cross the street, it takes her all day.'

'Rave on, Samson!' Mrs Clay called from the back.

Suddenly he hit the brakes again. 'There!' he said. 'That's my work right there!' He pointed proudly to a dumpy little bar-room bearing an artistic inscription on the outside wall: MIXED DRINK – FOOD – COLD BEER *whisky by the drink*. Other signs followed in wearying succession, all of them in more or less the same style: florid, highly visible, workmanlike. It was like driving around Chicago with Mies van der Rohe, looking at Barcelona chairs. 'Now I'll show you a beautiful job, an elaborate sign.' JOYCE'S BARBER SHOP, *specializing in processing, shoe shine*, done in silver-white and red, and topped off with a portrait, painted right on the inside of the glass, of a well-groomed dark-skinned man with a handsome head of hair. 'Now I'll show you some big work.' PACIFIC PLYWOOD PRODUCTS CO. 1299 12*st. the plywood supermarket*. 'This one Rudolph and Cassius

helped me on when Cassius was sixteen.' RENN'S AUTO
PARTS. 'Look at that work. Ain't that beautiful? That's
Persian blue with white lettering.' KING KARL'S THREE
ROOMS OF FURNITURE, on Market Street. A. B. HARRIS
M. D. DELIVERIES AND FEMALE DISORDERS, on Dumesnil
Street. Signs and signs and signs, the monuments to his
name, scattered all over town. We drove until dark, the
horn still honking willy-nilly, the rasping noise still
coming from under the hood, Cassius Sr still chattering
away about the homes he planned to buy, 'set back from
the road two hundred feet,' Clay Kitchens, Clay Enterprises, the one-man show of his paintings, the imminence
of Judgment Day, the dozens of relatives he would put
to work, the glory of the name Cassius Marcellus Clay,
and the vast promise of the future.

Odessa sat in the back quietly.

Part Three

THE WEIGH-IN CEREMONIES FOR THE FIRST CLAY–LISTON heavyweight championship fight were a mess from the beginning. Clay, then a twenty-two-year-old man-child, had a long record of disturbing the peace at such events. For weeks before the weigh-in, he had been conducting a loud, tasteless 'psychological campaign' against Liston, whom he called 'the big bear', and as the fight approached his tone had grown more and more hysterical, aggravated by predictions that he would be lucky to get off with his life. Everyone with half a brain knew that Clay would stage some kind of Cecil B. DeMille production at the weigh-in. This, of course, did not include the Miami Beach Boxing Commission, which arranged a setting that was an absolute guarantee of disaster. As William Faversham, who was then functioning as Clay's 'manager' on behalf of the Louisville Sponsoring Group, observed later, 'All they should have done was weigh the fighters in and get them out of there. But they made a great event out of it. They had the scales up on a platform and a chair for each fighter and the doctor was going to make his medical examination right up there on the platform. This was ridiculous, because it just kept the two of them together that much longer.' Said Gordon Davidson: 'It was so badly handled by the commission. They must have had five hundred people crowded into this one room, like a Roman carnival, women and men and sightseers and Roy Cohn in his bathing suit, hangers-on, King Levinsky selling ties and the whole bit. A bad set-up.'

Both Faversham and Davidson, in their roles as boxing figures, were reminiscent of the cartoon showing the Martian asking a jukebox, 'What's a pretty girl like you doing in a joint like this?' Faversham is a distinguished-looking man in his fifties, a Harvard alumnus, the son of a legitimate actor and a one-time actor himself. He is vice-president of Brown-Forman Distillers Old Forester, Early Times, *et al.*). Davidson, attorney for the Clay sponsors, is a Yale man who worked as Supreme Court Justice Stanley Reed's law clerk and became a tax lawyer and a respected member of Wilson Wyatt's law firm: Wyatt, Grafton and Sloss. Nowadays, Faversham and Davidson find themselves looking back with more and more wonderment on those years when they were escorting the brash young Cassius Clay from fight to fight around the country. 'What we were doing at the Miami Beach weigh-in was mostly worrying,' said the big, jovial Faversham in his gravelly voice. 'It has its elements of humour now, but I can tell you: at the time, it was no laughing matter.' Indeed, the arrival at the weigh-in of Clay and his court jester pro tem, Drew 'Bundini' Brown, was the beginning of a twelve-hour time of trial for the two professional men from Louisville.

'Clay walked in wearing his blue denim bear-hunting outfit,' Davidson recalled, 'and he was hollering, 'I'm ready to rumble!'' The two of them, Clay and Bundini, kept walking around the weigh-in room till somebody shooed them to the dressing-room. Faversham called me to the platform and he said, "Gordon, go back to the dressing-room and tell Clay that if he causes a scene they're gonna fine him, and it's gonna be his money, not ours. Tell him to behave himself."

'So I go to the dressing-room and there's Bundini, Rudy Clay, two or three other yucks and Angelo Dundee. Clay's lying down on a rub-down table perfectly relaxed. I said, "I got a message for you from the corner." I said, "If you go in and cut up they're gonna fine you, and it's gonna be your dough and they're gonna hit you pretty good."

'He says, "Don't worry about it. I'll take care of it." So then Bundini starts, "Well, they can't fine him! They can't fine the greatest!"

'I said, "Yes, they can, and he can pay!"'

Out on the weigh-in stage, Faversham fretted. 'I was wringing wet waiting for them to come out,' he said. 'And then we found out that both fighters were dressed but each was refusing to leave his dressing-room till the other did. So I went back to Clay's room and I said, "Look, Cassius, you're not the champ yet. When you're the champ you can come out last."

'He said, "I won't go in there unless he follows me right away. If he keeps me waiting I'm not gonna put up with it."

'I said, "Cassius, you have my word that as soon as you get on the platform Liston'll come in." I tell you, it was worse than handling Caruso!'

Lawyer Davidson, trying to look dignified, preceded Clay and Bundini out of the dressing-room, 'and as soon as they saw the crowd they started,' Davidson said. 'Clay and Bundini were shouting at each other, "Float like a butterfly! Sting like a bee! Ready to rumble! Let's take on the bum! He ain't no champ, he's a cheese champ!" Then when Liston came in with his great stone face, Cassius started, "You! I'll take you on right now! I can beat you anytime, you chump! You think you're something and I'm nothing!" And it reached a higher and higher pitch. I was standing in the back and Teddy Brenner, the promoter, said, "My God, he's scared to death." Brenner said he hadn't seen anybody so scared since one of Joe Louis' opponents could hardly answer the bell for the first round. He said, "This kid is out of his mind! He's scared. He may not show up for the fight!" Then Cassius said, "Hold me back, boy!" and tried to get at Liston. Faversham thought it was the real thing and he was trying to hold Clay, screaming at Clay. Bill's secretary was there, and we both thought he was gone; he'd had a bad heart.

'I was holding Clay around the waist,' Faversham recalled, 'and Sugar Ray Robinson was holding his right arm, and Bundini was against his back and whispering in his ear, "Float like a butterfly. Sting like a bee." I said, "For Christ's sake, Drew, shut up, will you?" '

Dr Alexander Robbins, the commission physician, said, 'Clay was acting like a maniac. I tried to tell him he was going too far, sweating and getting overheated, pulse rate going up, burning a lot of energy. I don't give a damn how strong a fellow is, there's a limit to how much activity he should undergo before a fight. He was acting like a nut. Getting attention.'

'So the commission announces a twenty-five hundred-dollar fine and Cassius finally rants and raves his way out the door,' Gordon Davidson said. 'I followed him to his dressing-room and he was sitting there and he says, "How about that?" And I said, "Well, it cost you a twenty-five-hundred-dollar fine, that's how about it." He said, "Oh, don't worry about that!" ' (Ultimately the commission settled for a thousand dollars, with Clay's sponsors paying the fine.)

Soon the captains and the kings departed, Clay and his entourage to spend the last hours before the fight in his little bungalow in north-west Miami, Faversham and Davidson to gobble a hurried lunch at their hotel. Said

With 'Mascot' Stepin Fetchit

Cassius Clay with Mama

Faversham: 'We were just starting to eat when a couple of British reporters came running up and said, "We hear the fight's off. The commission doctor says his pulse and blood pressure are way up." I had been afraid of something like this. So I went over to the Miami Beach auditorium as fast as I could and I found Angelo Dundee and Clay's doctor, Ferdie Pacheco, and I asked them to find Cassius and check his pulse and temperature. Forty minutes later the doctor called me and he said Cassius was lying on the floor at his house with about seven kids, all of them watching TV, and he couldn't be calmer. Blood pressure and pulse were normal. I said, "Stay there for the rest of the afternoon and double-check him every hour." What I was afraid of was that the promoters were trying to get out of the fight because the house was scaled so high and the sales were bad.'

The physician who made the journey to Clay's house that afternoon has seldom been quoted in the literature on Clay, despite the fact that he studied the loud young fighter the way some researchers worked on paramecia. Research into the genus *pugilismus* is the consuming hobby of Dr Ferdie Pacheco, so much so that he administers to the medical wants of about a dozen boxers, including Clay, for nothing. A balding bilinguist with a fine Spanish patrician face and a successful practice largely among Miami's Cubans and Negroes, Pacheco has been in the corners of Luis Rodriguez and Florentino Fernandez and Douglas Vaillant, not to mention Cassius Clay. The doctor is a fight buff, a movie buff, an art buff and a conversation buff. He enjoys batting the breeze with all human beings, but especially with boxers, and his relationship with Cassius troubles him. 'I don't have any idea why he comes to me in the first place,' Pacheco said, 'because I have no rapport with him like I have with anybody else. There are two or three coloured doctors in the same neighbourhood I'm in and they'd be highly honoured to have him as a patient. It must be that the price is right with me. I never charge fighters. I'm paying the muses. I like boxing.'

Pacheco had had no idea what to expect when he hurried to Clay's house in response to Faversham's request. 'The commission doctor had said if his heart rate and blood pressure were still running away at fight time the fight would be called off,' Pacheco said. 'So when I got to his house there he sat sipping tea, cooler than anything. It was impossible to believe. That little house was jammed with people, and after a while he says, "I think I'll take a nap," and he goes in his bedroom and sleeps all afternoon with a house full of people!'

In the years since Clay pulled his magic quick-change mood reversal, capping the performance by coolly defeating Liston that night, dozens of theories have been advanced by students of behaviour – from psychologists to bartenders. There were reporters on the scene who will go to their graves convinced that Clay was in a state of temporary lunacy, self-induced or otherwise. Some, like commission doctor Robbins, swung around to the idea that the whole commotion was an act, to which others responded: how can an actor make his heart rate double and his blood pressure jump so high that experts fear for his welfare? Some stuck doggedly to the position that Cassius was plain scared at the weigh-in and was trying to bolster his courage. Cassius himself said that he was just trying to annoy Liston, and knew what he was doing at every second. In Dr Pacheco's opinion, almost all of the theories had elements of truth in them. According to him, 'Everybody was trying to gauge Clay's emotions by a set of scientific criteria – blood pressure, pulse, respiration – that had nothing to do with it. He *wanted* to go there and raise hell and act like a crazy wild man. Now that's gonna alter your emotions no matter if you're Sigmund Freud or who you are. If I start

98

hollering at you and pushing you all over the place and jumping up and down, my blood pressure's gonna go up whether I'm faking my anger or not, especially if I'm doing all this in front of five or six hundred milling, pushing people and especially if I'm running the risk of getting smacked in return. You create the aura of hysteria and you're *hoping* that it gets you out of control. That's Cassius. He finally got himself into the fight-or-flight aspect of the nervous system, when you're either gonna fight or you're gonna run. The adrenalin flows and constricts all the blood into the muscles where you need it for action, and the blood pressure goes up because all the arteries are clamping down and the blood is forced through smaller canals, and the heart is beating faster to pump the blood: a state of alteration of body physiology.

'Now the more Clay did this the more he looked like a scared kid, like somebody walking the plank. He finally got himself into such an untenable position that it was a case of either beat Liston or really go down to oblivion. It was the act of an impulsive person who deliberately puts himself into a horrible position. In the same situation a common-sense person would sit back and say "Well, I don't want to go out and say I'll beat this guy real bad because *he* may beat *me*. I'll say he's a great fighter in case he beats me, and if the best happens and I win, I'll be a good winner and say the other guy was a hell of a fighter."

'Cassius did everything the opposite of that. He raised so much hell. Of course, he might have done himself some accidental good. Liston has this monolithic brain. He didn't know what to make of Clay. Liston is afraid of no man, but he may be the type of person who is superstitious or scared of insanity. You can predict what any sane man is gonna do in a competition, but not an insane man. And Cassius may have made Liston begin to wonder.'

Later on the day of the fight, Cassius made even Dr

Pacheco wonder. 'As fight time got closer and closer, Cassius still appeared very calm, but what did seep out as an indication of anxiety and nervousness was a very inexplicable distrust, a deep-seated distrust of anybody around him except his brother Rudy. And all of a sudden Angelo became suspicious to Cassius, and I became suspect, and he didn't quite trust the Cuban masseur, Luis Sarria, who is about the closest thing to a gentleman I know. It started as we were talking on the lawn, standing around waiting to get into cars to go to the auditorium for the fight. Cassius told me vaguely, "I don't trust you. You want Liston to win and you bet with gangsters," or something like that.

'I said, "Cassius, I'm here as a doctor. I'm not interested in betting."

'Then he turned to Angelo and he said, "I don't trust Mafia people. You're a bunch of Italian Mafia people." I was looking for him to be kidding, but he was deadly serious.

'Inside the dressing-room at the auditorium no one was there but Cassius, his brother Rudy, Angelo, Sarria and me and maybe Jimmy Dundee, Angelo's brother. Cassius started looking at his water bottle. You know, the bottle that's filled with water and then taped up to the top and taped over the cork? He said to Rudy, "You keep an eye on that bottle and don't let anybody touch that bottle." A little later Cassius takes his eyes off the bottle and he comes back and he says, "Anybody touch that bottle?"

'I said, "Who the hell's gonna touch it?"

'He refilled it. He must have checked the water bottle at least three or four times that night. He was insistent that somebody was gonna drug him. I told him if I wanted to drug him, I'd have done it long ago. He kept taking off the cork, refilling the bottle and emptying the bottle again. He did this three or four times. And I kept

looking at Sarria and saying, "Who does he think? . . . '
and Clay's muttering about people trying to do him in,
as though somebody was trying.'

This was not the first time Clay had shown distrust of
medical men. He has always seen doctors as frightening
figures, and he made no exception of Pacheco from the
beginning of their relationship six years ago. 'He would
go to any length to avoid being treated,' Pacheco said.
'Once he developed an abscess, an infection, on his leg.
It could have been a hazardous thing because an abscess
can go into the bloodstream and cause all kinds of trouble,
even in young people. So here he has a great big throbbing
abscess for days and days and he's still out doing roadwork, still sweating into it, and not getting any treatment.
I finally had to lance it and put a drain in it.

'And whenever I've ever had to give him a needle I've
had to chase him around the room. He just keeps moving
like somebody doing the rhumba. And he'd talk: "What
are you gonna do? Show me what you're gonna do. Show
me that needle. Don't touch that! Wait a minute! Let me
look. Wait, wait, wait a minute . . . " That would go on
ad infinitum till I'd tell him to shut up and turn and look
at the wall, and then I'd go *zonk*.'

After several years of studying Clay at first hand,
Pacheco became convinced that the fighter was suffering
from anxiety, not old-fashioned fright. 'Fright's too
strong a word to use about Cassius,' the doctor explained.
'Anxiety is what he has: an unconscious fear of nothing.
The difference is, if a man's chasing you down the street
with a hatchet, you have fear. If you're running down
the street and you *imagine* a guy's chasing you with a
hatchet, you have anxiety. Cassius isn't afraid of being
hurt by the other fighter. He just has an anxiety about
everything around him. His position in life depends on
his winning. His looks depend on his not getting beaten.
He purposely walks the plank to the very end while

somebody's sawing it off, and he's got to beat up the guy before he finishes sawing it off, and fortunately he has the ability to do it.'

Something vaguely similar to Pacheco's plank-walking or brinkmanship analogy seems to recur in Clay's dreams. 'I'll be on the highway,' Cassius recounted, 'and I'm running head-on at a diesel truck doing seventy, eighty miles an hour, and people's stopping and looking, and just before the truck hits me I jump up and fly on over it, spring off my feet and jump over it and land behind it.' And again:

'I'd tell everybody, "I'm gonna fly up in the clouds," run down the street and tell everybody. Then I'd run up a great big old tall building. I'd be out on Times Square, on top of the Empire State Building or sumpin', and everybody'd be looking at me, thinking I'm gonna kill myself. Thousands of people around looking up, firemen and policemen coming, trying to talk to me through this big old loudspeaker. "DON'T JUMP! What are you trying to do? Come down! What's wrong?" And I'd say, "I'm getting ready." I'd get everybody on edge, and then I'd jump off the building and just stop in the air, just flap my wings like those little birds you see on Disneyland, just stop in mid-air, and everybody'd be fainting and looking and saying, "Ooooooooooooh!" Then I'd fly back to the building. Then I'd run real fast and jump way off, and just fly and float on down and land on my feet. Then I wake up.'

'That dream is important to him,' said a friend of the champion. 'He's told me about it a half a dozen times, and the way I got it figured is maybe that dream tells him he can keep on going, keep on pushing yourself and pushing yourself, you'll come down on your feet. You can do anything. But deep down inside I think he's plain scared of a lot of things.'

By his own admission, Cassius is beset by fears, some

more real than others. But he is not willing to accept the hypothesis advanced by his former boxing coach and others that his raving and railing before fights is simply a way to get up his courage, to charge his emotional batteries. 'Falsehood!' says Cassius. 'Falsehood! It's just my way of looking at a fellow and worrying him, to bother him. And it gets the people interested in the fight too. Builds gates.'

Patrolman Joseph Martin goes back the farthest of anyone involved in Clay's career, having steered the fighter from bird-legged novice at twelve to Olympic gold medal winner at eighteen. 'He's been popping off before fights from the very beginning,' Martin said, 'and it's not a thing in the world by whistling past the graveyard. He'll build himself up till he gets in a regular frenzy. He's just overcoming that fear that's in him. He has a certain amount of dog in him, and I'm not saying that to knock the boy, either, because I had a very enjoyable time with Cassius, and I have no animosity toward him whatever. We're all afraid of one thing or another, and it takes a brave man to fight to overcome his fear. Cassius' way is to make a lot of noise and commotion. He was always a loudmouth, liked to talk, but of course I kept him curbed. When I thought he was talking too much, I made him shut up. I have complete discipline over all fighters that I've handled. 'Course, sometimes I'd let him pop off to another fighter if I thought it'd do some good. He'd psych a lot of fighters. He'd tell each opponent what he was gonna do to him, and it bothered plenty of 'em.

'But sometimes he went too far and annoyed everybody. When we were at the Olympic trials in San Francisco he popped off a lot the night before the finals. He was popping off so much that the people booed him some. I sat him down in the hotel before the finals and I said, "Tonight you're gonna sit down and you're gonna keep your mouth shut because if you don't I will take you out of the Olympics and you won't even fight in the finals!" and I wasn't kidding. And he knew that I meant it. And he went there and sat down and he was very nice.'

Once Clay was training in Chicago for an inter-city Golden Gloves match and the coach threatened to send him back to Louisville if he did not pipe down. 'I wasn't with him because the inter-city team was being coached by another man,' Martin recalled, 'so they phoned me in Louisville and had me straighten him out over the phone. He was a light-heavy at that time and the mistake he was making was he was popping off to the heavies.'

No one appears more upset than Cassius when an opponent has the poor grace to become angered by this pre-fight gamesmanship. He acts as if the opponent is violating the rules of the fighters' union. 'They're supposed to take it and roll with it and realise that it's more than half baloney, as Patterson and Liston did,' said Gordon Davidson, who has been an uncomfortable spectator at many of Clay's performances. 'He'll make some very pointed remarks, do some very insulting things, too. Like when Liston was talking at one of the signings? Cassius pretended to fall asleep and he snored loudly. But Liston understood this and made some nasty remarks back and it didn't make Cassius mad.'

At the Charlie Powell weigh-in in Pittsburgh, Clay's barbed tongue brought him close to a showdown, bare-fisted fight, although there are differing versions of the incident. According to the most popular of the published versions, Clay flailed away at Powell with insults, and Powell took them seriously and threatened to fight Clay on the spot. When Clay saw that he had enraged Powell, the atmosphere changed. Clay backed off, lost his composure, began to whimper and put on his sweater inside out.

Angelo Dundee tells a slightly different version of the

story. 'Cassius started telling Powell, "You're an old man. You're nothing. I can lick you."

'I was afraid because Powell's brother Art, the football player, was there, and he began to get hot, and he said to Clay, "I'll knock you . . ."

'I told Powell's brother, "Cool it!" I said, "We're just having some fun and we're trying to sell some tickets," and we did, too. It was twelve below zero that night and we sold out the place.

'Anyway, Charlie Powell's a good talker, too, and he's telling Clay, "Look, I'll beat you like I'm your daddy."

'Cassius had predicted a knock-out in five and so he said to Powell, "Now I'm gonna cut it to three 'cause you're popping off! There's no room for two pop-offs in this business. I'm the pop-off!"

'But I don't think Charlie Powell ever got mad. It was his brother. He couldn't fathom what was going on. Football's not like this, Art was really steamed. He was gonna take a poke at Clay, but I cooled him off. People said Cassius was afraid, but he wasn't. Nothing disturbs him. He's the master of all situations. Nothing bothers him. He may pretend that it does, but it doesn't.'

Clay does admit to a certain antipathy toward genuine, bare-knuckled fisticuffs, a feeling that goes back to his early childhood. He hated street fighting and avoided it enthusiastically. 'I never did bother nobody,' he said. 'Didn't want to get hurt. You can get hurt, killed, fighting with rocks and sticks. We'd have these fights on the way home from school. We'd be running and they'd be trying to get us, just like cowboys. I was afraid of a lot of those kids, the ones that was a little bigger. They didn't do nothing to me, really, but I wasn't no champion in those days. I didn't know nothing about boxing.

'The first day I enrolled in junior high school I was coming home. And there was two boys, one was Dub Jr and one was Toady Moe, and they looked tough at that time. They walked up to me and they said, "Gimme your money!"

'I said, "I ain't got no money."

'I don't know if you ever experienced this or not. That's the way the big ones were. "Bring me a ham sandwich tomorrow!" they'd say. I was scared!

'I said, "Man, I gotta go get a ham sandwich!" Sometimes I wouldn't come to school. I'd duck. Or I'd slip out the back way and run home.'

'I'm a peaceful person,' Clay said on another occasion. 'I can't remember ever getting into a fight, a real fight, when I was a kid.' He was reminded of a time in junior high school when a boy swung a T-square at him. 'Oh, yes,' Cassius said. 'That was my onliest fight. He called me sumpin' and I said, "Don't you call me that!" and he came at me with the T-square, and I blocked it with my arm and hit him in the jaw with my right hand and knocked him out. But I didn't *like* that kind of thing!'

The galloping contradiction implicit in the Clay who needles his opponents and the Clay who dreads coming to real blows was painfully obvious during his campaign to goad Sonny Liston. The two met briefly in a Las Vegas casino and Clay began to ridicule Liston in front of a crowd. Sonny had endured this sophomoric hazing process several dozen times before, including an early morning visit of the whole Clay entourage to the Liston home in Denver, and he did not mind going along with the gag in order to build a gate. But this time Cassius caught Sonny in a grouchy mood. He did not feel like being ragged, and he invited Clay across the room for a private discussion. One report said that Liston 'fixed him with a long, murderous look, then slapped him sharply across the face,' whereupon Clay said, 'W-wha' fo' you do that?' and walked out. Even the kindest version of the incident, the one told by loyal Angelo Dundee, includes the information that Liston slapped Clay, although

Angelo said 'it was more of a pat, a gesture.' All versions have Clay beating a retreat.

'The odd thing about Cassius is that he sees the world around him as a hostile environment,' said a Louisville friend who had known the fighter since childhood, 'and he goes out of his way to make it more hostile by rubbing it the wrong way. Even when he's talking about race – when he says, "I don't want to be bombed, I don't want to be set on fire, I don't want to be lynched or have no dogs chase me" – he's expressing more of a general fright than he is a real racial attitude. I think he finds it safer to be with Negroes, his own kind. It allays his fear of all those things his father used to tell him the whites'd do to him. He keeps this tight little Negro group around him and he's scared to death to venture away from it. I think if you scratched down deep enough, you'd find that was at the bottom of the whole draft thing. You notice how he really blew his cool when he was first reclassified? The idea of going in the Army with all those strangers, to put himself into that strange environment, with *white* people at that – man, that really hit him where he lived! For a while there he was almost hysterical about it, like he was scared to death. That was the *real* Cassius Clay!'

Figuring out who or what is the *real* Cassius Clay is a parlour game that has proved unrewarding even for experts. Clay's personality is like a jig-saw puzzle whose pieces were cut by a drunken carpenter, a jumbled collection of moods and attitudes that do not seem to interlock. Sometimes he sounds like a religious fanatic, his voice sing-song and chanting, and all at once he will turn into a calm, reasoning, if confused, student of the scriptures. He is a loudmouth windbag and at the same time a remarkably sincere and dedicated athlete. He can be a kindly benefactor of the neighbourhood children and a vicious bully in the ring, a prissy Puritan totally intolerant of drinkers and smokers, and a teller of dirty jokes. 'They say there's fifteen sides to Clay,' said Dr Pacheco. 'To me he's just a thoroughly confused person. Sure, he has sides, but they don't mesh like the sides of a Borgia or a Cardinal Richelieu. There's no cohesion of thought from one personality to the others. He is capable of all kinds of paradoxes. He hangs around with Stepin Fetchit, making a mascot out of him. Now, can you imagine a Black Muslim, someone with all their racial aggressiveness, can you imagine one of them making a pal out of the top Jim Crow symbol of all times! If ever there was a character in the world that the coloured people should want to bury, it's Stepin Fetchit. But Cassius couldn't see any contradiction in that. There's so many other paradoxes about Clay. Take the verbal barrage he unleashes when any reporter comes close to him and his reticence when you're talking to him man to man. He's not a verbose person except when he's in a crowd or talking to a reporter. And nobody ever talks *with* Cassius. You listen *to* him. This man who's known all over the world for his mouth can't even converse. You don't get an exchange of ideas. He doesn't even hear you.

'And take his sense of humour. He's got a strange insight into humour, when it comes to making things up about himself. But person to person he's humourless, devoid of it. He can't see humour when it hits him in the face. He never catches wit; he always takes it seriously.'

Clay's jokes are often on a fourth-grade level. 'Why'd the bus driver drive his bus off a cliff?' he asked a captive audience in Miami. 'To test his air brakes.

'If you had a gun and a mean old police dog was coming at you from one side and a panther coming at you from the other, which would you shoot first?' he went on. 'Give up?'

'The panther?' somebody offered.

'No, you fool!' Clay chortled. 'The gun. You'd shoot the gun first!'

Cassius uses jokes in the same way he uses poems and bizarre statements: to keep the centre of the stage. He is utterly unselective about his audience, so long as there is one. He is like an old ham actor who can no longer discuss, only orate, whether addressing an audience of thousands or the garbage man over the back fence. Huston Horn described a taxi ride with the young Cassius in Louisville:

'I wonder what my mother is doing with my Cadillac this morning,' he says in a loud voice. The cab driver doesn't hear. 'How much did that watch cost you?' he asks his companion. Cassius confides that when a wrist-watch was given him recently by a Negro civic club in Atlanta he found a concealed price tag. It cost only $49.50. He mentions it because, gift or not, it didn't cost enough. He rambles on in a loud voice for the driver's benefit: 'Sure is a pretty day; day just like this I won that gold medal in Rome last summer . . . Reminds me of the day they had the parade for me in Louisville, too. The mayor, everybody was there, man, to welcome me home. Then I went up to Frankfort to see the governor.' When Cassius still gets no rise from the driver, he tries a joke he has heard from another boxer. 'One day I was fighting Sugar Ray Robinson. Man, I had him scared silly for for two rounds. He thought I was dead.' The driver is silent and Cassius looks out the window, glumly.

Clay is puzzled by such indifference because he thinks of himself as a credit to Louisville and easily the town's most distinguished citizen. 'He thinks that he put Louisville on the map,' said Joe Martin, 'that no one had ever heard of Louisville till he came along.' Clay goes to great lengths to preserve an image of himself as a historic personage. Back in the days when he was travelling about in a little red bus, he had 'World's Heavyweight Champion' lettered on the side (by his father, the sign painter), but one day he confided to a friend: 'Maybe I better buy me some paint and a brush. Then if the bus broke down I could quick paint out my name on the side. That'd be embarrassing for folks to know the champ's bus had broke down.' When the bus did break down, Cassius stood off to one side and said in total seriousness: 'My poor little red bus. You was the most famousest bus ever in the history of the world.'

'He believes anything about his own greatness,' said Dr Pacheco. 'He's a narcissist. He loves himself above all people. You get to such a withdrawn state in narcissism that you love yourself at all times. You'll notice a narcissistic woman is always touching herself, looking in mirrors, clutching at herself, smoothing her skirt, and all unconsciously, unaware. Cassius is the same way. I think if you went up to Cassius and said, "If you could change yourself physically what would you change?' he'd say "Nothing." He likes everything about himself. Sugar Ray Robinson was another narcissist, but he had an intelligence and a polish about him that Cassius just doesn't have. As far as physical equipment is concerned, Cassius is damned near perfect. You can hardly blame him for being narcissistic. And on top of that he's a good-looking fellow, and when he wants to be, he is charming and personable enough, especially when he puts on that little-boy attitude of his.'

'You never know what to expect of him,' said a Louisville friend. 'He's completely unpredictable. Like when he used to come here with that bus of his. He'd go out and collect twenty-five or thirty kids, put 'em all in that bus and ride 'em around. Stop at the ice cream place and buy 'em all ice cream, and then they'd drive around singing at the top of their lungs. I never could figure it out. Normally you'd expect a guy like Cassius to be struttin' around with his peers.'

There are times when Clay attempts to picture himself

as a man of peace and kindness, a man who was accidentally shoved into the cruel sport of boxing. 'When I run over a dog I feel bad,' he said. 'When I shoot a bird I feel bad. I feel sorry for everybody I beat. I feel sorry for Liston. I don't like to hurt people. I don't like to fight, except for making a living and providing the good things in life.'

And yet there are times when his opponent in the ring seems to infuriate him, and for no particular reason. In Miami Beach he worked out often with Mel Turnbow, a six-foot five-inch 230-pounder who speaks in monosyllables and shuffles around like a sleep-walker, expressionless and withdrawn. 'I feel sorry for Turnbow,' the gentle Angelo Dundee said. 'He lives in a world of his own. He ought to talk to people more. When you get him to talk, you find out he's a sweet and inoffensive person.' Clay did not treat Turnbow as one would treat 'a sweet and inoffensive person'. Sparring one day with the huge Ohioan, Clay suddenly went down under a barrage of punches. He wobbled to his feet and was knocked down again, and lay on the floor with his eyes shut and his mouth open. Turnbow stood confused and embarrassed, and finally turned toward cornerman Solomon McTier as though imploring his assistance. Suddenly Clay, who had been faking all the time, reached out and grabbed Turnbow by the ankles, spilling him to the canvas while the crowd roared its laughter. For the rest of the sparring session Turnbow seemed to bring out a vicious streak in Cassius. He would let Turnbow hit him for a minute or two, then suddenly mount an attack that would have the big man gasping. Turnbow stood in the middle of the ring, almost a stationary target, while Clay ran around him with his Fancy Dan footwork and poured punches on the almost defenceless sparring partner. Angelo Dundee finally hollered 'Time!' and told Clay that Turnbow had had enough. The same pattern was repeated on other days. Cassius would box carefully and skilfully with Jimmy Ellis or his brother, Rudolph Valentino Clay, but the big Turnbow would incite him to riot, and he would forget all about finesse in a kind of wild drive to knock the big man out. One member of the Clay entourage thought he understood. 'Turnbow lives back at the house along with Ali and all the rest of us,' he explained. 'But he doesn't take part in anything. He doesn't look at the television with Ali; he doesn't laugh at Ali's jokes or tell him how great he is, and at the dinner table he just eats and doesn't say a word. This is the one thing that bugs the champ the most – to be ignored. And he'll dislike anybody he thinks is ignoring him.'

Clay's closest relationship is with Rudolph, the quiet, brooding, fiercely handsome younger brother whom many see as a sort of *éminence grise* behind the champion, laughing childishly at everything Cassius does but skilfully pulling the strings on many of his moves. 'Rudy is the ornery one of the bunch,' said a former neighbour of the Clay family. 'He has genuine hatred in his soul for white people, and Cassius does not. I think it was probably Rudy that helped Cassius get into the Black Muslims. They know for a fact that even though he's a couple of years younger than Cassius, Rudy was in the Muslims before Cassius was.'

As a boy, little Rudolph did not enjoy the neighbourhood popularity of his big brother. 'He was a funny kind of kid,' said an older man who lived on the same block. 'He liked to fight, and he'd even jump on Cassius and try to whup him. Fighting, crying, fighting, crying, that's all Rudolph ever did! But one thing about him: he had the guts to stand up against his father when the father was hard on the mother. Once when the old man really teed off, Rudy let him have it good. They had to move Rudy over to stay with friends for a couple of days, till the whole thing cooled off. Rudy told his father he wasn't gonna have it no more.'

The parents seldom mention Rudolph; in many ways, he has become the forgotten child, with so much attention focused on the noisy older brother. 'Rudy was such a baby,' Mrs Clay said one day in a rare comment about the newly re-named Rahman Ali. 'Hanging around me when he was little.'

'Yeh,' said the father. 'He a mama's boy!'

'Young Cassius'd go out painting with his father,' Mrs Clay said, 'because he knew his father would keep buying him things to eat all day long.'

'That's right,' said Cassius Sr. 'But when Rudy'd go, by the time I'd get ready to work he'd be saying, "I wanna go back to mama, I wanna go back to maaaaamaaaaaa. 'Course, he was younger'n Cassius.'

Rudolph's relationship with Cassius, always close, grows stronger with the years, and one seldom sees one without the other. 'I think he's the greatest,' Rudy said worshipfully. 'He's the greatest man there is, because he's my brother and we're very close, and he's a wonderful brother, very good-hearted and helpful. I'm thankful to have such a brother.'

The boys' aunt, Mrs Eva Waddell, mother of six children by vocation and professional haircutter on the side, wrote years later about the childhood of the two Clay boys:

'Cassius was inseparable from his brother, "Rudy". If Rudy wanted to sit in the back seat of the car Cassius would sit with him, the same thing happened with the front seat. Sometimes five children were in the car but it was always the same. He seemed to think Rudy was his little brother to be taken care of as such and he would put his arms around Rudy as if Rudy was his baby.'

For several years, young Rudolph emulated Cassius in the ring, fighting first in the amateurs and then on under-cards of his big brother's professional fights. Rudy's pro career began when he fought and defeated a tough boxer named Chip Johnson the same night Cassius defeated Sonny Liston for the heavyweight championship. Cassius watched nervously as Rudolph pounded out a win, taking some punishment along the way. After the fight, Cassius said excitedly: 'You're never gonna fight again, little brother! I'm gonna win this championship, and you're never gonna have to fight again. I'm gonna take care of you for the rest of your life. You ain't got nothing to worry about. Ain't no brother of mine gonna go out there and take a whuppin'. You just sit right here and you be my sparring partner and you help me and I'll take care of you the rest of your life.' Soon after, Rudy's pro career ended.

Dr Pacheco witnessed the scene in the dressing-room and said about it later: 'The whole thing was very touching. Here Cassius was getting ready to fight the most important fight of his life and he was mainly worried about his brother. I thought it was all very nice, a laudable thing about Cassius.'

Rudolph's idolatry of his older brother is often mistaken for sycophancy, which it is not. 'Those two boys really love and admire each other,' said Angelo Dundee, 'and if you mess around with one of 'em, you're gonna have the other one on your neck in a second.' When Cassius works out in the gym, Rudy stands nearby admiring every move his brother makes. One day he watched Cassius hitting the speed bag and examined the technique like an art student watching Picasso stippling. Cassius hit the bag for ten minutes and Rudolph never took his eyes away from the scene. 'I can understand Rudy learning something, some little thing, by watching his brother hit the speed bag,' said an onlooker in the Fifth Street Gym, 'but what's he learning now?' Cassius was getting rubbed down by the Cuban masseur, Luis

Sarria, and Rudolph was studying the process. When Clay worked a few rounds with the speedy light-heavyweight James Ellis, Rudolph watched from the corner. 'He's even too fast for Ellis,' said a ringsider, trying to make conversation with the taciturn Rahman Ali.

'He fast,' said Rudy, without turning his head from the ring. 'He fast. He fast. Fastest there ever was.'

A Louisville radio and TV personality told of an early radio interview with Cassius: 'After that show a lot of people asked me what Cassius thought was so funny that he kept laughing all through the show. I told them that wasn't Cassius laughing. That was his brother Rudy they heard.' A recorded radio interview with Cassius produced a steady droning in the background, which turned out on playback to be the younger brother muttering 'right' every time Cassius opened his mouth.

The two brothers have become so close that it is difficult to imagine their going separate ways. Rudolph is married and living in Chicago, and Cassius spends much time at the house. Cassius plans to marry eventually, and, according to Rudolph, 'He and I and our wives are gonna live in the same house. We want our children to be close.' Said Cassius: 'That's right. He's my onliest brother, and I got to take care of him.'

Like their father, both the younger Clays do not count policemen as their best friends, tending to get their backs up whenever they encounter the law. Rudolph's contacts have been few, and limited to traffic violations, but Cassius has been in various minor scrapes and usually manages to turn simple offences into highly publicised cases fraught with overtones of civil rights and injustice to minority races. Twice he has had his driver's licence lifted for accumulated offences, and at least a half dozen times he has been fined. He has even been subjected to the indignity of being clapped in a paddy waggon and hauled down to the police station for booking on a charge of disorderly conduct. The scene was Chicago's South Side, in a neighbourhood where a Negro is more or less presumed guilty until proved innocent, so far as the average policeman is concerned. Clay and two other friends were in a borrowed Cadillac driven by a man named John Cage, who turned out to have a long police record including twenty arrests for robbery and narcotics. Two detectives noticed that the car bore no licence plates and ordered the driver to stop and the occupants to get out. One passenger, who identified himself as Omar Bey, twenty-two, of Miami (and who formerly had been known as Ronald 'Tuddie' King, a childhood friend of Clay from Louisville), shouted to the detectives: 'You can't stop this car. Cassius Clay is in here!'

Clay himself said, 'Do you know who I am?'

A detective said, 'No,' and Clay said, 'I'm the champ.'

The plain clothes men asked if the men carried any weapons, and Clay said, 'No, I'm a Muslim.' When the detectives started to pat him down, Clay said, 'Lay a hand me and I'll put a brutality charge on you!' He said that he could not be arrested because 'I represent another government.'

'What government?' asked one of the detectives.

'The Negro government,' Clay snapped. 'I'm a fifteen-million-dollar-a-year man and you're nothing but a policeman. The only reason you arrested us is because we are Negro.' Minutes later, the whole assemblage was en route to headquarters in the back of a paddy waggon, with Clay raving at the policemen: 'You want a white champion. You'll never get one. Nobody is going to beat me!' He told reporters that he became angered when the detectives started to search him for weapons. 'They tried to pat me all over like I was a gangster or something. They were hostile, they paid me no respect.

If I was Ingemar Johansson or Rocky Marciano they wouldn't be patting me around like that. I don't want to be no national scandal. I don't drink, don't smoke and don't run around with women. I'm trying to be clean.'

One of the arresting officers explained, 'We tried to treat him like a gentleman. But he was lippy. The other men acted like gentlemen.' Three of the arrestees, including Clay, were charged with disorderly conduct, and one, presumably a man of rare courtesy and statesmanlike charm, was released without charge. Cassius put up a twenty-five-dollar bond and went back to his hotel to receive the news that the New York Boxing Writers had just named him 'Fighter of the Year'.

'That whole incident was totally unnecessary,' said an old friend of the champion, 'and I can't help but feel that Muhammad was slightly at fault himself. It would make anybody mad to be driving along peaceably one minute and be standing out on the street getting frisked the next, but Muhammad should know that that's just one of the hazards of being a Negro on the South Side. What was his crime? Talking back to a policeman? Well, who is a policeman that you can't talk back to him? Is he God or something? The sad truth is you got to kowtow to these cops down here even when you're in the right. It's just a fact of life and Muhammad should have watched his lip. Who does he think he is, a white man or something?'

According to Ferdie Pacheco, many of Clay's characteristics grow out of his tendency to be contrary or 'oppositional'. 'He longs to figure out what the public expects him to do and then do something else, even if it's the wrong thing sometimes,' the doctor said. 'Lyndon Johnson has a slight tendency the same way, and so do a lot of us.'

When Clay announced that he was going to apologise to the Illinois Athletic Commission for his remarks on the draft, and then flew to Chicago and refused to back down, he was behaving contrarily and typically, just as he was when he came out for the Doug Jones weigh-in with a two-inch swatch of adhesive tape over his mouth. After the Boxing Writers Association voted Clay fighter of the year and asked him to make an acceptance speech at a banquet, Cassius spent two hours brain-trusting in New York's Americana Hotel with his brother Rudolph, Angelo and Chris Dundee, Black Muslim Potentate Herbert Muhammad and eight or ten others. At Clay's request, they were trying to figure out what the writers expected Cassius to say, so that he could say the opposite. The result was a modest, gracious speech in which Clay, for the first time in his life, gave public credit to the men around him and asked each to take a bow. For a while the boxing writers thought they were looking at a new Cassius Clay, but it was the same old model, striving for effect, seeking to confuse and confound the menacing world around him.

Part Four

TO A MIND LIKE YOUNG CLAY'S NOTHING JUST *happens*. There are cabals within cabals, and the biggest plotters of all are the whites, all whites, keeping the Negro on his knees. 'If you want to know how that kind of thinking gets started,' said a friend of the Clay family, 'go out and ask his father how he feels about the Pope. Then you'll get an idea of what Cassius was brought up on.'

'The Pope?' said Cassius the elder, huffing and snorting like a bull coming through the tunnel to the ring. 'Lemme tell you about the Pope. Ummmmmmmm. *Ummmmmmmm*. About eighteen years ago, maybe longer'n that, twenty-three and a half years ago, Rome was in a war with Africa. Am I right? Ummmmmmmmm. Now hold still now! The Africans were barefooted. They didn't understand. They were fighting with spears and things. The Roman people went over there and trapped 'em in a big place with barbed wire around it. Burned 'em up!'

He was asked what the Pope had to do with his story.

'What did the Pope have to do with it!' Cassius Sr said as though he were talking to an idiot. 'The Pope is the leader of Rome. The Pope got a *lot* to do with it. He's the head of the Holy City, man!'

The elder Clay finds himself in an impossible situation nowadays. The Muslims have ordered young Cassius to

119

stay away from his father, and the father has to try to convince his son that the Muslims are wrong in order to win him back. But Cassius Sr's arguments about race and Elijah Muhammad's arguments about race sound almost identical (*e.g.*, Muhammad on the Pope: 'The late Pope John who recently died, according to history, used to be a soldier and then a general. He fought in wars and did many other acts of unrighteousness before taking his place at the head of the church.').

Cassius Sr has always found it difficult to mask his suspicion and distrust of anyone lighter than he is. 'You gotta watch people all the time, study 'em,' he said. 'I'm not like Cash. See, my daddy was an iceman. He got around a lot, and the white man'd come into the coloured people's houses and fall up in the beds, lay up on the beds, and a white woman wouldn't let me in the front door and ask for the insurance money, and the coloured door. You follow? White man'd come to the door and ask for the insurance money, and the coloured lady'd say, "I ain't got it," and he'd holler at her, "Why ain't you got it?" He'd come in her house and boss her even! And I'd say, "Man, I wish that was my house, I'd put that sum bitch outa there." Wouldn't you? I gotta go in that white people's house by the back door, and then the white man comes bossin' in the front door of the coloured! That's the way it used to be when I was a kid. And it wasn't so hot around here when Cassius was growing up, either. The white people in Kentucky do things on the sly that they wouldn't do down in Mississippi. They more sly here and on up north. I'd rather they'd dome to my face than slip around my back cuttin' me up. See, they're deceitful. In the south at least they come to your face and stab you. Am I right?' He laughed loudly at the comparison.

'One of my clients said one day, "Why don't you come inside and eat with us?" And I said, "No, I'll eat out here.

I don't like that deceit." He said, "How come you don't want to eat with us, you think you're better'n us?" I said, "No, sir, you white people so deceitful." I told another one how the white people'll go to church on Sunday and then go out and hang somebody on Monday.' This, of course, is exactly the line followed by Elijah Muhammad and the Muslims; the sins of some whites are visited upon all.

The elder Clay's thoughts are often tuned to violence, and after he has had a few drinks he will spin horror stories about the injustices inflicted on Negroes around Louisville, leaving one to wonder how many similar speeches must have fallen on the ears of Cassius Jr as he was growing up. 'On Seventh Street one day,' the father said, 'there was a little coloured boy about seven, and a white girl about the same age. He asked her for a cigarette or something like that, and these two white guys came out of this truck and took a chair and beat that coloured kid to death! Killed him! Ain't that something to think about, man? Just for talking to a white girl! No, I never told Cassius *that* story. I wouldn't tell him that for nothing. You'd *never* get him out of the Muslims if I told him that story!

'But he knew about things like that. They killed a coloured boy here, what I call a "legal lynching". Now just hold still. A nice-looking boy, twenty-one years of age, going with a white girl at General Hospital. Something came up, the white cops caught 'em together, and they said to her, "We're gonna disqualify you from our race," and they said, "You love a nigger and you're going to court and you better say he molest you." And they burn that young boy. Charge was rape. Artificial rape. A legal lynching. The girl came back the day before he was burned, and she said, "No, he didn't rape me, we was going together." And they said, "It's too late now." Happened about fifteen years ago. Cassius knew about it.

'When I was a boy, seemed like every darned day you'd read in the paper about something like that: a lynching, a burning of a Negro, every day. Now wouldn't that turn you against the white man? Nine or ten or twelve or fifteen cases like that a week?'

Considering Cassius Sr's description of the Louisville of his own youth, his son's early life seems to have been fairly free of racial incidents. According to the parents, Cassius' first awareness of colour came when he was three years old. His mother, the light-skinned Odessa, recalled, 'One day he said to me, "Mama, is you a white lady or a coloured lady?" I said to his father, "How did he know enough to ask sumpin' like that?" And later on when he was about four, he said, "Mama, when you get on the bus, do people think you a white lady or a coloured lady?" I was shocked! I said, "He's too little, how he know the differences in colour?"'

Soon after, the boy began asking his father about race. 'When he was five years old, he said to me, "Daddy, I go to the grocery and the grocery man's white. I go to the drugstore and the drugstore man's white. The bus driver's white. What do the coloured people do?" I just explained to him there was more opportunity for the white people, that they rule everything.'

Father and son told me curiously contrasting versions of what appeared to have been the child's only physical brush with the race that 'ruled everything'.

'A white man grabbed Cassius when he was about five, six years old,' the father said. 'This big old sum buck gonna pull him into a car, gonna snatch him. I got so damned mad, I said, "You turn that little boy loose." Cassius had been playing on the railway tracks by the granary, and that big old sum buck was roughing him around, beating on him. Somebody came to us and told us the guy was beating him, pushing him around. I made him back off. Cassius was crying.'

Said the son: 'Yeh, I remember sumpin' like that. There was a little sand and rock granary alongside the railway tracks. We'd jump off the roof into the sand pile and this man'd come out and chase us. There was a little hole in the concrete wall leading out of the place and I was running through the hole and he caught me by the collar and dragged me. And he said, "I'm gonna give you a good whippin'." I started hollering and he said, "Shut your mouth, little nigger! Shut your mouth, little nigger, I'll give you a good whippin'." Some man came along and said, "Let that kid go!" He let go and said, "Get on outa here quick," so I did. I was eight or nine.'

('Oh, he was kicked around when he was a little boy?' said Clay's laconic Aunt Mary Carter when she was asked about the incident. 'Well, aren't we all kicked around, and don't we kick 'em back? Most of the time you just kick 'em back or hit 'em or something. If it had been my child and some white man picked him up off the railway tracks and stung him, I'd say good, 'cause a train could have done it. It's according to how you look at things. Sometimes people just want to blame their shortcomings on somebody else. They blame it on you and when you're gone they blame it on me!')

Cassius Sr remembered taking his wife and two sons to the Kentucky State Fair when Cassius Jr was about six. 'We got in line to see something,' the father said, 'and I told them, "You all are first now. Stand right there! Don't let nobody get in front of you!" And a white lady heard me and she said, "Lookee here! You're still down south! You still in the south!" It's things like that's the trouble with Cassius now.'

And when Cassius was younger, the father went on, 'We were downtown and he said, "I want a drink of water." And his mama said to me, "You know they're not gonna give him no drink of water in downtown Louisville!" And I said, "Sure, they would." I said they may be illiterate and ignorant and animals, but they wouldn't turn no baby down when he wanted a drink of water. Wouldn't you say the same thing? So we asked this girl at the ten-cent store and she threw up her hands and she said, "I'd lose my job!" ' '

Cassius Jr did not remember the water incident, but he listened enraptured as it was recounted to him second-hand. At the end, he said, 'That just backs up why I'm a Muslim. Imagine! There I was, a little bitty baby, a little brown baby in Kentucky, with a nice mother and a father that loved everybody, worked honest, wasn't asking for no pistols to go steal, which as the first law of nature he could have done. We're in the shape where we could pick up arms, but we don't.' He started slowly, but in reconstructing the story with all its racial harmonics he seemed to get carried away. 'Now here's my mother, a pooooor humble sweet Christian. This is what Christianity done for the Negroes. She don't hate nobody, love everybody. My father just don't do nothing but stay around and paint, play with the birds, a humble man. He don't think evil against nobody. Now here they've got a little bitty baby boy who's destined to be the champ of the whole globe in his own little country hometown, and all he wants is some water. This is the work of the devil the way the white do! This is a little baby who is just thirsty. He don't know what he's in the world for. Don't know nothing about colour. Mama and Daddy wasn't asking for something that couldn't be done.' He went on and on, his voice rising and falling, his face showing sorrow and anger, in a regular Dostoevskian dirge. 'The baby was just thirsty, and all the little baby wants was a drink of water. If he went down the street somewhere and died of thirst, they wouldn't want him to do that. If he just drinked the water out of the gutter or the rain off the roof he might catch a disease. He might die or catch a hospital bill. But all the little baby wanted was a drink of water and they wouldn't give the baby no water . . . Poor old Negroes, worked and slaved three hundred and ten years for his master, loved his enemy, and they shoot 'em down in the streets in the north and the south just for asking for justice. Lynch and tar-and-feather 'em, pour alcohol on 'em for three hundred and ten years! You'd think that God wouldn't let them continue misusing his humble people like this.'

Clay sat on the edge of his bed in Miami, shaking his head solemnly from side to side, and a stranger might have guessed that he was on the verge of tears. But after a small amount of contact with him one learns that he is a ham actor first and a suffering Negro second; he spins out long laments about incidents he does not remember, all the while casting sly looks at the listener to see what impression he is making, and if he is not moving his audience sufficiently, he works doubly hard, wringing his hands and making his voice quiver with emotion.

Cassius claims that the white race is obsessed with guilt about the Negro, and in order to prove his point he puts on a performance, a sort of one-man happening, in which he plays all parts including sound-effects man:

'A house is on fire, pretend. You're sleeping next to your partner. [Sound: snoring.] You open one eye and you see the house is on fire. Your partner's still sleeping. [Sound: snoring and whistling.] And you see this hot lava and this burning two-by-four is getting ready to fall on your partner, and you get out of the bed. You run out of the house without waking him up!

'When you get outside, you say [clasping hands and looking skyward], "Oh, Lord, what have I done wrong? I was so selfish and greedy and worrying about myself until I forgot about my partner inside. Oh [wringing hands], he's probably daid, the house caved in."

[Dramatic pause.]

'*And then he comes out just in time and he looks you in your face!*

'Right then you feel he's supposed to kill you. You know what *you'd* do if somebody left *you* in a burning house. Right then you feel he's supposed to hate you because he would have a right to hate you. And he says, "Man, why didn't you wake me up? Why did you let me stay in that house? [Shouting.] THE HOUSE WAS ON FIRE! MAN, YOU WERE GONNA LET ME BURN! WHAT'S THE TROUBLE WITH YOU, BUB?"

'Right then you'd take the defence. You'd say, "I didn't know, I didn't mean it. Don't kill me!" You feel like he *might* kill you.

'Well, that's what white Americans are like. The house's been on fire for three hundred and ten years and the whites have let the blacks sleep. The Negro's been lynched, killed, raped, burned, dragged around, all through the city, hanging on the chains of cars, alcohol and turpentine poured into his wounds. That's why the Negroes are so full of fear today. Been put into him from the time he's a baby. Imagine! Twenty-two million Negroes in America, suffering, fought in the wars, got more worse treatment than any human being can even imagine, walking the streets of America in 1966, hungry with no food to eat, walk the streets with no shoes on, existing on relief, living in charity and poor houses, twenty-two million people who faithfully served America and who have worked and who still loves his enemy are still dogged and kicked around . . . '

Cassius Clay's attitude on race is a tangled confusion of truth, half-truth and untruth based on hatred and distrust of the oppressing whites and pity and compassion for the victimised Negroes. He claims to believe literally that all whites are devils, and challenges any 'whitey' to prove otherwise. He looks with contempt on racially relaxed athletes like Floyd Patterson and calls them 'white men's niggers'. He is firmly dedicated to segregation, and he believes that God, or 'Allah', is on the side of the black man and will cause the downfall of the United States before long.

'Negro is a name meaning something neutral,' said Cassius the preacher, 'neither forward nor backward, like you take a car and put it in neutral and it's just settin' still. And that's the way the American so-called Negroes are. We don't have no factories. We wear shoes every day and we don't make no shoes. We wear shirts every day and we don't make no buttons. We eat three times a day and we don't grow no food. If the white man took back everything that he made, Negroes wouldn't have no clothes, wouldn't have no food to eat. So we just a nation depending on another nation – a neutral. And we haven't progressed no farther than we have a hundred years ago. A hundred years ago almost all Negroes had a job, but today we can't even find jobs, and this is 1966. Automation and the time we living in makes us in worser condition than we were a hundred years ago, I would say, and this is only me talking, remember. Financially and jobwise we're dead. We've been made dead socially, morally, spiritually, culturally, financially and economically. So we fit the description of dead people, and that's what Negro, *nekros*, means in Greek: it means something dead.'

To some extent, all of Clay's beliefs grow out of his own personal pride and his reactions to early indignities suffered at the hands of white people in his home town. These earliest ideas were reinforced by simple lessons in hate learned in childhood and by advanced lessons in hate learned at the feet of his surrogate father, Elijah Muhammad, leader of the Black Muslims. And Clay's anti-white position was consolidated intellectually by certain unfortunate social truths about white Americans and their relations with other races.

As in many other matters involving the heavyweight champion, the mystery is how the intensity of his feelings was kept hidden for so long. Until the draft situation fanned some of his anger and made him reveal himself at least slightly, Clay's public image had been that of a naïve young man who was being led to parrot racist remarks, but who underneath it all loved mankind, whites included. Every time he took an anti-white step, such as his move to divert theatre TV revenues into the Black Muslim hate group, his close admirers explained that Cassius meant no harm. 'Cassius love all people,' said his mother. 'He's just that type of person.' And Aunt Coretta said, 'How Cassius could wind up with people like the Muslims is just one of those things you can't comprehend. But I really know that Cassius isn't like that. Any white man that walks up the street now and says "Hello, son," he'll shake hands with 'em and have words with 'em.' What she did not add, and perhaps did not know, is that a few minutes later Cassius might be expressing the most intense loathing for the white race, including the stranger whose hand he had just accepted. As long ago as 1962, young Clay was showing his true feelings. He and his brother Rudy spent a day in Louisville with a white writer, Roy McHugh, and McHugh discovered in a barber shop mirror that the brothers were making derisive gestures toward him when they thought his back was turned. Later Cassius developed an even deadlier technique toward whites: he became capable of looking at them as though they were not there, of staring them straight in the eyes while they were asking questions and then pretending that he had not heard a sound. In other words, he learned to treat white men as many white men treat Negroes.

Much of Clay's theorising and philosophising about race comes dangerously close to the outermost limits of reason, and much of it is pure balderdash, straining one's credulity. Sometimes it is almost impossible to accept the idea that he believes what he is saying. Sometimes he

Cassius in action against Brian London

With the late Malcolm X on the lawn of Clay's Miami home

(Photo: Tony Triolo)

sounds as though he is trying to convince himself, and at other times he sounds like a young Marcus Garvey leading black folks toward the boat for the trip back to Africa. 'Once a man learns nature and culture he wants to be with his own,' he will chatter, 'and he's not comfortable with anyone else.' If you disagree, he is likely to show annoyance. After I had spent an enjoyable morning with him, sitting in his house and listening to tales from his childhood, I told him, 'I don't understand why you say whites can't be comfortable in Negroes' houses. I'm in your house and I'm comfortable.'

'You understand it!' he snapped. 'You're just playing dumb!'

Then he launched into a lengthy explanation: 'The white man has always had a white restaurant and a coloured restaurant at the railway stations, and even in New York they got a place called Harlem; and in Chicago they got a place called the South Side. It'll always be that way and a man who has a knowledge of hisself *wants* it that way. He won't want to marry a white woman. He'll want to keep up his race pride. White people want to stay white. We honour that. But we just want to stay black.

'I didn't always feel that way. I used to have a saying: "I will pay a white woman's way to California and back but I won't even tell a Negro how far it is." I used to say a Negro woman can't do nothing for me but show me which way the white woman went. I'm showing you how I was brainwashed and thought that white was prettier than my kind. I used to say if I ever got to be champion I'm going to London, Rome, Paris, I'm gonna have a good time over there. Over there we can be around white people and integrate and have no trouble. I was *so* sick! That's the way Negroes think, even now. A Negro woman in Chicago just took her children to Sweden. Why didn't she take 'em to Ethiopia, Ghana, Nigeria?

E

'You got to love your own kind. I just love my people and their children. I hug the little Negro children when they come around the yard. They're so humble and sweet when they come around and they don't bother nobody. They don't have a future, and nobody really teaches 'em the truth. I couldn't feel the same way about a white child, not like I love my own colour. I wouldn't feel like hugging and kissing a white child 'cause he's not my kind, and then later when he gets bigger he'll have to turn away from me or else give up everything he's got just to be with some poor Negro. He's got brothers and sisters and friends that'd condemn him for being with me. Kennedy got killed, Lincoln got killed. They meant right, but they were surrounded by the other whites.'

I argued that there were more and more whites who lacked prejudice and that the historical trend was toward tolerance, but I added: 'Judging by the way you're talking, I don't expect you to believe me.'

'I believe you,' Cassius said. 'If we just had a lot more white people like President Kennedy and the few that I meet that are real sincere, things'd be better. Even if every so-called Negro could find just one white that really was different, well, that would be twenty-two million, that would be a lot of 'em. And if every Negro found two decent whites, that'd be forty-four million.' Suddenly his expression changed from a sort of dreaminess to an artificially hard look, as though he realised he was ranging far away from the Muslim line. 'Trouble is,' he said quickly, 'I've never even seen ten decent ones get together.'

Clay reserves his choicest invective for Negroes who refuse to draw a colour line and live by one. He might grapple such persons to his soul for brief periods, perhaps in an attempt to reform them, but ultimately they will be cast out. One such was Drew Brown, the fascinating

'Bundini', who trained Clay for a few fights and brought zest and merriment to the champion's camp. The beginning of the end for Bundini came on a private bus trip from Florida to New England, one of those wild odysseys so characteristic of Clay's life. Because there were reporters like George Plimpton and Edwin Pope aboard Big Red (Cassius' nickname for his bus), the incident is fully documented, and remains one of those rare peep-ins at southern ignorance and shame: a cameo of prejudice. The bus was moving through the pine forests of northern Florida in the dead of night when Bundini, always the one who provided the momentum for the champion's activities, suggested, 'Let's stop and eat. I'm empty.' The next town was Yulee, and the driver, a Muslim, turned the bus into a truck stop with a small adjoining restaurant. Rudy Clay, then known as Rudolph X, peered out the window and said, to nobody in particular, 'You're going to watch a man face reality – that's what you're going to see.'

Bundini and four reporters walked into the place while Cassius and the rest stayed behind, back near the petrol pumps, to watch. Bundini's delegation walked through a squeaking screen door and into a small room where a half dozen couples sat eating quietly in booths. Bundini and the reporters took places at the counter, and within seconds the manager was standing in front of them. 'I'm sorry,' he said sheepishly. 'We have a place out back. Separate facilities. The food's just the same.' He smiled. 'Probably better.' Bundini's face showed annoyance, but he said nothing. The white reporters began arguing. The manager tapped the menu against his fingertips. 'In this county – Nassau County – there'd be a riot,' he said.

'The heavyweight champion of the world,' said Bundini, 'and he can't get nothing to eat here.' He stood up just as Clay came through the screen door shouting.

'You fool – what's the matter with you – you damn

fool!' Cassius raged. 'I told you you ought to be a Muslim. Then you don't go places where you're not wanted. You clear out of this place, nigger, you ain't wanted here, can't you see? They don't want you, nigger . . . ' He gave Bundini the bum's rush out the door and on to the macadam, then gave him an extra push toward the bus.

'I'm glad, Bundini!' Cassius shouted, running around the petrol pumps like a wild man. 'I'm glad. You got *showed*, Bundini, you got *showed!*'

Bundini looked like a man in shock, his eyes staring down at his shoes. 'Leave me alone,' he said over and over. 'I'm good enough to eat here. I'm a free man. God made me, not Henry Ford.'

Cassius laughed loudly and jumped in the air. 'Don't you know when you not wanted?' he cried. 'Face reality and dance!'

'I'll be what I was,' Bundini said, 'what I always been – in my heart I'm a free man. No slave chains 'round my heart.' He ran into the bus.

Rudolph X said, 'A man has seen reality, seen re-a-li-ty.' Cassius took a seat behind Bundini and the bus eased back on Route 17. Hardly had it pulled away from the pumps when Cassius began berating Bundini again. 'Uncle Tom!' he shouted. 'Tom! Tom! Tom!'

When Bundini tried to answer, Clay muzzled him with a pillow and said, 'This teach you a lesson, Bundini! You bow your head, Bundini.'

'Leave me alone,' Bundini said. 'My head don't belong between my knees. It's up in the stars. I'm free. I keep trying. If I find a water hole is dry, I go on and find another.'

'You shamed yourself back there,' Cassius said.

'*They* were ashamed!'

'What good did that do, except to shame you?'

'That man, that manager,' Bundini said. 'He'll sleep on it. He may be no better, but he'll think on it, and he'll be ashamed. I dropped a little medicine in that place.'

'Tom! Tom! Tom!' Cassius screamed, smacking Bundini with the red pillow. 'You belong to your white master.'

Said Bundini: 'To a fool it may seem like that! But to a man who's been around the world he know the world is a black shirt with three white buttons.'

'Bougainville!' Cassius said, referring to one of the battlegrounds of Bundini's World War II service. 'If I hadn't pulled you out of that place back there, those crackers'd killed you!'

By now Bundini had all he could take, and he began to cry. At first Cassius kept hammering away – 'Why you want to go in places that don't want you? Why you want to be white? That's why I wouldn't go in there, because I knew something like that was gonna happen. Bundini, you ain't nothing but a nigger! You were born a black nigger and that's all you're gonna be is a black nigger. You and your white wife and your white friends, see where they got you!' But when he saw that Bundini was quietly sobbing, Clay said softly, 'Hey, Bundini.'

'Leave me alone,' Bundini whispered.

Clay tried several stunts to make Bundini talk again, and when nothing else worked, he said, 'Hey, Bundini, what sort of crackers was they back in that restaurant?'

Bundini said nothing.

'I'll tell you what kind of crackers. They was *soda* crackers. And if they're soda crackers, that makes you a graham cracker. That's what you are – a graham cracker!'

Cassius began hitting Bundini on the head and shoulders with the red pillow, and soon Bundini was shaking with laughter. 'Champ,' he said, 'let's just train and fight – none of the other stuff. Why you make us come this way? We could have flown over all these miserable miles.'

'Don't fly over it, Bundini. You fight it out, Bundini,

like your aunts and uncles have to do.'

A little later Bundini said, 'I'm empty. I want to eat. A Howard Johnson's coming up.' By now the bus had crossed the state line, into Georgia, and Cassius said, 'We'll stop. This is Georgia, Bundini. You haven't been *showed?*'

The Muslim driver parked the bus in the Howard Johnson lot and the group split into two contingents: Bundini, the reporters and several of the sparring partners strode briskly up the walkway toward the restaurant, and Clay and the rest of the Muslims stood alongside the bus. Rudolph called out a parting shot: 'You facing reality, Bundini,' he said. 'Reality!'

The eating group walked directly to a large table and sat down, waiting for the trouble to start. A waitress handed out menus and said, 'You all look hungry!'

Bundini began to laugh. 'My,' he said, 'no one mind if I sit at the head of the table?' He looked out at the Muslims. 'I'm going to eat three steaks standing up so's they can see,' he said. When Cassius walked in a few minutes later, Bundini said, 'What you doing here? This place only for integrators.'

Cassius sat down, ate his meal and ordered coffee. 'Bundini,' he said, pouring the cream, 'I'm going to integrate the coffee. When it's black, it's strong!'

The battle was over, and both men smiled, but the fundamental differences between them remained. Not long afterward, Bundini was out as Clay's trainer and court jester. 'I don't need no comedian no more,' Cassius explained tersely. Nor did he need a reasonable man.

Cassius Clay's proudest claim is that 'black is best', although he once thought otherwise. 'I used to think black was bad. My mother and father used to tell me if I go in this dark room the bogeyman would get me, and he was black. A black cat was bad luck, little black ducklings on the TV cartoons always walked in the back and had the hard time. And then I heard Muhammad's teachings and I found out that black wasn't bad, black was the best. Which is stronger, black coffee or white coffee? Which make better crops, black earth or light earth?'

He uses the word Negro, but only as a convenience; he prefers the simple word 'black' and wants to be known as 'an Asiatic black man', even though his ancestors were Africans and white Americans. Caucasians who do not understand how he came to be an Asiatic black man and not a Negro are shrugged off as simpletons, but Negroes who argue the point are likely to be treated as traitors. Once he was debating the subject on Milton Metz's conversational radio programme in Louisville. A telephone caller said, 'I would like to know: a few minutes ago you stated that you are not a Negro.'

'No, ma'am,' said Clay politely. 'Not a Negro.'

'Well, I would like to contradict you.'

'Yes, ma'am, start contradicting.'

'And I have proof of this.'

'Well, prove it.'

'I am a Negro and proud of it,' the lady said.

'Well, I am proud I am a black man and I am not a Negro.'

The caller said, 'Now the word Negro comes from a Latin word *niger*, which means black.'

Clay began to show a slight testiness. 'Well, why don't you say, why don't you say, why don't you say colour in English and quit going to Latin and saying black? Do you say *niger* shoes? Do you wear a *niger* dress, *niger* pants, *niger* shirt? If it is black, you call everything black in English, but when it come to your name you go to Spanish. You is a black woman! You *are* a black woman! I said I am a black man.'

'The English word Negro is derived from the Latin word meaning black,' the caller went on. 'It is a dead language which is no longer in formal use. But many of our words stem from it . . . '

As she spoke, Cassius began to build up a full head of steam, and finally he exploded: 'I think when you call for debate you should get real versed because you have just been proven wrong right now over the whole radio. You a Negro – or Niger or whatever it is – if it means black, two thousand years ago . . . I don't want to know nothing about two thousand years ago! I am speaking English today. I am a black man. Don't go to that language to get the word black! You call your dress black, you call your pocketbook black. Why don't you say you got a Negro pocketbook or a Negro dress? So you're hypocritical! You ashamed to say you black!'

'No, I'm not ashamed that I'm black. I am telling you what is right. You say you're a black man. And you are a Negro.'

'Negro comes from a Greek word called *nekros*,' Clay said, 'and *nekros* means something dead. I am not a Negro. You see, Chinese are named after China; Cubans are named after Cuba; Russians are named after Russia; Hawaiians are named after Hawaii; Indonesians are named after Indonesia; Algerians are named after Algeria; Ethiopians are named after Ethiopia; Indians are named after India. So what country is named Negroes?'

'Okay, all right, but what about—'

'Okay, I am not a Negro. I am Muhammad Ali. It is the black man. And I am an Asiatic black man . . . Woman, go back and get versed on what you talking about. Next person!'

Moderator Metz tried to spray oil on the troubled air-waves, but Cassius sputtered angrily. 'This was one of my people who is a so-called Negro. All the whites are calling me, giving me respect, following me by my name,

(*Photo: Fred Kaplan*)

Cassius at home

Angelo Dundee (*left*), Clay and William Faversham (*right*)

(*Photo: Tony Triolo*)

and when I explain things to them they have enough common sense to use simple facts and reasoning and say, "Champ, that made sense." But here's a so-called Negro – one of my kind – who I am defending, standing up for, calling me and debating and trying to say that I'm crazy for saying what I'm saying when all of the people of the other race are saying that they understand. "Champ, it makes sense. You have made it plain." But they won't argue. But you notice there is always some – I am not saying this about this woman – but it is always a fool to fight truth.'

In more private conversations, Cassius is apt to be less tolerant of the whites and much less complimentary. Like his father, he takes a conspiratorial view of history, and he charges the white race with pulling off some anti-Negro coups that would never have entered the imaginations of Leroi Jones or James Baldwin in their angriest moments. Young Clay offered to bet a Louisville reporter one hundred dollars that Barry Goldwater would win the 1964 presidential election, and explained that Goldwater was anti-Negro; therefore the election would be rigged in his favour. Who would rig it? the reporter asked. 'The whites,' Cassius said.

He is also convinced that white Americans are engaged in a conspiracy to use big-name Negroes to brainwash Negro children. As he explained to a Negro friend in Miami, 'Jackie Gleason's trying to show me why I shouldn't be a Muslim. He said, "Champ, why don't you think about it?" He's not the onliest one. All the big whiteys are trying. They want me to be their nigger. The whites made all the big niggers rich. Like you take all the big Negroes – Lena Horne, Eartha Kitt, Diahann Carroll, Chubby Checker, Sammy Davis. Take those big niggers Floyd Patterson, Sonny Liston. The whites make 'em rich, and in return they brainwash the little Negroes walking around. Liston lives in a white neighbourhood,

Patterson lives in a white neighbourhood. Liston carried a little white boy right on his knee, promoting a little white boy. I carried a little coloured. I can live in the Fontainebleau, anywhere I want, but I live here in a slum with my people. I could have taken money from the whites, but it would brainwash all the little black children.'

'I was in an integratin' in Louisville, Kentucky,' Clay once told me, positioning Louisville geographically for about the hundredth time in our acquaintanceship. 'It was at Central High School, and I went downtown to march and integrate.' His face showed that he meant this story to be funny. 'And I got some hot water poured on me that day!' He laughed, but I did not join him; so he started over. 'I was mad because we couldn't go to the white shows. I was mad because the white girls wouldn't look at me. Sure, I was in an integratin' demonstration. I wasn't famous then. And a white lady poured hot water on me!' He shook all over with laughter.

'Boiling water?' I asked.

'Yeh,' he said, barely able to speak. 'Hot boiling water!' More laughter.

Then he pulled himself together and said, 'Man, I said to myself, "Whoo-OOOO! This water's hot!" I said to myself, "Sumpin's wrong, this ain't right!" I said, "Sumpin's gotta be better'n this integratin'!"' He jumped up to laugh in a standing position, and I asked him why the woman had singled him out for the hot water. 'Why me?' he said, shrieking and giggling. 'Why *not* me? A nigger's a nigger!' He rapped me on the back as though enjoining me to come on and laugh; he would not be offended. 'A nigger's a nigger,' he said again, and stumbled into the bathroom to wipe off the tears falling down his face.

As a result of all Clay's histrionics, his use of racial stories to move his listeners one way or the other, one is never sure to what extent his reminiscences are exaggerated, understated or perhaps completely apocryphal, or even to what extent he may be kidding himself. Consider his straight-faced explanation of how he first came to realise that there was genuine black culture in the world:

'One time I was walking the streets of Louisville, Kentucky, and I saw two Africans black as coal, wearing their long robes. Turned out they went to the University of Louisville. They went into a movie show that I couldn't go into, and I waited till they came outside and I said, "How come you went in the show and I can't go?" And one of 'em said—' Here Cassius shifted to a clipped, staccato, tribal-African accent that would have done credit to a professional impressionist. ' "Well, mon, I hov my flog, I hov my longuage, I hov my religion, I hov my culture, I hov my name, and I om a Offrican." He say, "You don't hov your name, you don't hov your flog, you don't hov your culture. You're the white man's Negro." Then he walked right off.'

Cassius let that slightly suspicious story sink in, then rambled on: 'That started me thinking. Walking down the streets, the whites would look down on you, pass you up like you was a little dog or something walking around. They didn't look at you to be equal or to be a man. I knew I was the greatest, superior to anybody, best in my field complexionwise, features, health, good as any man or better. I said, "Something's wrong somewhere." And I laid in my bed many a night crying, and always wondering, "What can I do to help free the Negro?" I had dreams of walking up on God, and him telling me what to do. I always hoped that some miracle would happen that would change the Negro's condition. And I always had a feeling I was meant to do something divine, something that God wanted me to do, a feeling that I'm on some type of little mission, something to do with the freedom of the Negro in America. I used to walk down the main street in Louisville, Kentucky, looking at how the Negroes couldn't go to this show, looking at how the Negroes couldn't eat here, or how the whites'd look at 'em. After the Negroes had been working three hundred and ten years for America, working sixteen hours a day without a pay-day, fighting all the wars for America . . . And then I come back home with the Olympic gold medal and the light-heavyweight championship of the whole world, representing my country, America, coming back to this little city called Louisville, Kentucky, where I was born and raised, and then go to a movie or a restaurant and can't get served. I did this a lot of times. In the hot summer-time I'd go in an open door for a glass of juice, and they'd say, "Can't serve you." I went in one place and asked to be served and the waiter told the boss, "He's the Olympic champion," and the boss said, "I don't give a damn who he is, get him out of here!" '

In his earlier days as a travelling amateur boxer under Patrolman Joe Martin, Clay had handled the eating problem differently, although the same burning pride was motivating him. Martin recalled: On our tours we'd go into places where he wasn't allowed to eat and they'd tell him to leave. And he would take it very graciously. He'd just say, "Well, I'll wait outside, Mr Martin, and you can bring me sumpin' when you come out." Never one time did he get hostile. He's a firm believer if you don't want to associate with him, why, that's fine. I mean it don't hurt his feelings.' Once in his early pro years Clay and a reporter ordered root beers at a drive-in on a hot day. The white reporter was served in a frosted mug and Clay in a paper cup, and Clay did not show the slightest anger. 'Don't make trouble,' he said. In sub-sequent years, however, he referred to the incident so many times that one may draw the conclusion that he was truly shaken.

As a full-fledged practising Black Muslim, Clay was likely later to exaggerate such incidents as part of his continuing campaign to expose the whites as the devils Elijah Muhammad said they were. On his private bus ride from Miami to Boston just before the second Liston fight, he made a point of shouting loud, unsettling remarks about eating places, to the chagrin of a few Southern reporters who were aboard. 'You think we far enough up the road for a nigger to eat?' he said at Rocky Mount, N.C. Once he plopped into a seat next to columnist Edwin Pope, a Southerner who has an enlightened view about race and a genuine affection for Clay. 'He's so big he liked to squeeze me out of the window,' Pope recalled, 'and he starts right in with one of his race jokes. He says, "They've got this big restaurant at Kennedy Airport and this African came in and they served him and said, 'Where you from?' And he said, 'Africa.' And then a coloured Egyptian came in, and they said, 'Where you from, sir?' And he said, 'Egypt,' and they served him. And finally this nigger came in and they said, 'Where you from?' And he says, 'From right here in Brooklyn,' and they said, 'Well, you can't even sit down!' "

'That was the whole joke, and I just sort of sat there. It plain wasn't funny. And he repeated the punch line about five times and I still sat there. And he said, "What's the matter? Why ain't you laughing?" He's used to having that bunch of camp followers laughing at everything he says. So I said I didn't think the joke was funny, and he says, "No, you ain't laughing 'cause you know it's true! You know it's true, man!'

'I said, "Oh, cut it out!" I said, "I been listening to this for three days now, and it's beginning to wear a little thin on me." '

That was when Cassius was twenty-two. At the ripe old age of twenty-four, he appeared to have worked out a solution to the problem of eating, or not eating, with the white man, and he had a handy speech prepared for anyone who asked him about the matter:

'We Muslims are taught about our own food, the natural food for an Asiatic black man: Muslim-cooked food. After we learn that, we don't want to break down the doors of a white man's restaurant. Take the big meal I had last night: okras and tomatoes, fresh-cooked; squash, turnip greens, string beans, lamb chops, a big steak, bean soup, wheat break, all of that Muslim-cooked food. That one meal's enough to hold a man twenty-four hours. We Americans have a bad habit of eating three meals a day. This isn't good because our hearts have to work too hard to keep digesting. That's why I'm faster than any heavyweight in history, because I only eat one meal a day, according to Muslim teaching. That's why I don't get tired, because my heart is strong. It gets a lot of rest. Some days I do snack on a couple of eggs and toast and a glass of juice at breakfast time, but that's just like a coating for my stomach, that's all. And I never eat anything in the white man's places. And anyway I don't want a milk shake in a white store because they'll kill their own brothers to keep Negroes out, they'll close their restaurants to keep the Negro from coming in, they'll bomb their own place to keep a Negro out. Then they will spit in my milk shake and mix it up and I won't see it because I can't see spit in a milk shake. So I won't feel comfortable. I want to go in my own restaurant where my own beautiful women are there. I can play the jukebox and play James Brown, Sam Cooke, the Miracles, the Supremes, Ray Charles, the kind of music I like. If I see a girl I want to wink at, I don't have to worry about getting strung up to a tree or causing all kinds of race trouble! So I just want to be with my own!' This statement so excites him that he begins to sound like a tent-show evangelist, and he sums up his racial beliefs the way Bible Belt preachers and their sermons do, on a peak of feeling and bombast and gesticulation. 'Yes, I just want to be with my own! I now have a knowledge of myself! I'm no longer a Negro! I'm no longer dead! I'm no longer a Clay! I'm no longer a slave! I want to be myself and with my own kind! So therefore I get along with you better! Because now I know who you are! I know what you're like and I know who I am! So we will get along better!' And suddenly he is finished, breathing easy, cool as an oyster and waiting for questions.

I was impressed by this speech the first time I heard it. Here was bed-rock sincerity, the man's soul bared, a searing look at the true Cassius and his pride and his fears. But after I had heard him make more or less the same speech three or four times, I began to wonder if it was bed-rock Clay or something he was trying to drum into himself, a lesson he had learned by rote from the master. Then I began to notice that he has a package of these set speeches, and he keeps coming back to them, like a man whose whole philosophical outlook is poised on three legs, and if one breaks, all break.

He preaches the sermon that I've come to call 'Lions Stay With Lions and Tigers With Tigers', another entitled 'Twenty-two Million Poor Humble Negroes Who Faithfully Served for 310 Years', and a particularly fiery one called 'Back Home in Louisville with the Olympic Gold Medal'. When he takes off on one of these virtuoso performances, no one bothers to interrupt. His voice rises and falls, Holy Roller style; veins stick out on his neck; his volume and tempo increase rapidly and he races on to his conclusion like a runaway truck. And then the speech is over, and the coolest cat in the room is Cassius Clay, his passion turned off like a cold-water tap. The whole experience is like being back-stage for

143

the last scene of *Hamlet*. The audience is gasping; blood is being spilled all over the stage; everybody but the prompter is getting killed. And all at once the cast is lighting cigarettes and sending out for pizza.

This ability to switch instantly from a gallop to a walk, from violent excitation to complete equanimity, puzzles many of the men around Cassius, including several physicians. Minutes after his greatest road-show triumph, the weigh-in scene in Miami Beach when a commission doctor said Clay's heart and blood pressure were running wild and he was 'scared to death', the fighter was to be found stretched out on a sofa, relaxed and calm. 'How'd I do?' he asked friends. 'How'd I do?' It is the consuming question of his life.

Part Five

DRAMA WAS PILED ON DRAMA THE NIGHT CASSIUS CLAY
won the world's heavyweight championship from Sonny
Liston, and not all of it was in the ring. Dr Ferdie
Pacheco, Clay's personal physician, was sitting at ringside in the middle of a group of men with names like
Omar and Abdul and X, Black Muslims who were there
to cheer their number-one showpiece on to victory.

'You remember what happened after round four?'
Pacheco said. 'Cassius got something in his eyes and he
wanted to quit? He came back to the corner with his
eyes full of tears and Angelo Dundee did the natural
thing: he soaked a sponge in water and wiped Clay's
eyes with it. Well, when he did that these shock troops
around me started saying horrible things. One of 'em
said, "I knew a white man was gonna screw us!" The
white man being Angelo. And they said all these horrible
words because they thought Angelo had put something
on the sponge and *that's* what was making Clay's eyes
hurt. These Muslims were saying that they were gonna
get Angelo after the fight and beat him up and so forth.
So I hollered to Angelo, "Wipe your own eyes with that
sponge! Wipe your eyes so they'll see there's nothing in
it!" So finally Angelo wiped his own eyes to show them
the sponge was okay. Can you imagine? He didn't have
enough to do in the ring: he had to put on an act for the

145

shock troops. He *had* to. Those guys don't kid around. They'd already warned Angie before the fight: "Nothing bad better happen to Cassius." They gave Angelo an awful time.'

The Black Muslims, or 'the Nation of Islam', as they want to be known, profess to be non-violent, especially about wars, but their textbooks reek of violence. They forbid the carrying of weapons, but they have perpetrated at least one bloody assassination and almost certainly more. They reckon adultery one of the two worst sins, but their leader has been the subject of paternity suits brought by his teenage 'secretaries' and has been accused publicly of fathering eight children out of wedlock. And not the least of the Black Muslims' long list of contradictions is their acceptance of the heavyweight champion and their bestowal upon him of the super-duper holy name, Muhammad Ali. One would have presumed from the available literature that Clay would be near the top of the Muslims' white list. Elijah Muhammad has publicly gone on record against sport, calling it a 'filthy temptation' which causes everything from theft to murder.

How does a religion which regards sport as a 'filthy temptation' manage to embrace the world's best-known athletic figure? Elijah Muhammad does not condescend to answer such rude questions. Like his disciple Cassius Clay, he does not make conversation; he makes pronouncements. Clay himself offered this explanation of his acceptance in the inner circles of the Nation of Islam:

'When I first joined the Islamic religion and became a member I was already an established ranked pro. And this is the onliest way I have of making my livelihood. And some of our leaders mentioned that it would be bad for the public to be able to say that my religion caused me to be financially hurt and stopped from boxing.'

The Muslims soon went a step beyond this kindly tolerance. Herbert Muhammad, son of the leader, became

Clay's business manager and later his ring manager as well. 'I can't do nothing without Herbert's okay,' Cassius began telling business associates. 'See Herbert. He'll tell you yes or no.' Main Bout, Inc., was formed to handle Clay's theatre television rights, the biggest slice of the fight melon, with Herbert Muhammad as president and John Ali, national Muslim secretary, as treasurer. On the face of it, the move appeared irreconcilable with Elijah Muhammad's philosophy about sport.

'The truth is that the Black Muslim religion is about the most bendable religion in the world,' said a relative of young Clay. 'When they have got to choose between accounts receivable and the scriptures, they vote for accounts receivable every time. They thought sports was a mortal sin till Cassius came along. Now they're all running around in jock straps. They act like Cassius is Saint John or Saint Luke or somebody, but according to the Muslim beliefs, he ain't even a very good Muslim! Sometimes he talks foul, which is against their religion. He eats more than once a day, which is against their religion, and he makes his living from sport; shame! shame! They're getting a lot of mileage out of him now, but they'll drop him like a hot potato when he's outlived his usefulness to them. They're using Cassius, and he's too dumb to know it.'

'Look at it this way,' said Ferdie Pacheco. 'Before Cassius came along, the Muslims were a lunatic fringe type of idiots. They were running around saying things like "Kill Whitey!" and "Take 'em with you!" And none of the coloured people were paying any attention. The Muslims'd put up a sign that said "Mosque 29" and people laughed like hell and never went in. People were out looking for the action and the music and the chicks on Friday night; they weren't looking for Mosque 29 featuring women wearing dresses down to their ankles and nobody drinking or smoking or anything. That might make it in the Bible Belt in Ohio or someplace like that, but not in the coloured part of town. Now here comes the world champion and he's preaching the Black Muslim religion. And he's making it a big thing. Before he came along, you never even hears the Black Muslims mentioned.'

'There's only one reason why they don't throw him out,' said the champion's mother, Odessa Grady Clay. 'They want him for his money and his popularity.'

'That is correct,' said her husband. 'Muhammad using my boy and all the other people he's got. He preaches the whites are no good. Ummmmmmmmmmm. You take me. I know a lot of bad things the white man's doing, but I know a lot of good things he's doing, too. Now listen now! Ummmmmmmmmmm. Muhammad says the white man does all bad and he's got the solution. A separate land for Negroes. Like Marcus Garvey back in the Thirties and his Back-to-Africa campaign. That corresponds to the Black Muslims. It had the same motive: money. It's something that'll never come true, never gonna happen, it's impossible. Ummmmmmmmm. Whose material they gonna use, whose boats, whose money's gonna sail out? It's impossible. But they make a lot of money off it. Why don't these Muslims go down to Mississippi and do something? And fight! Now Martin Luther King went down there and faced those people, and the Muslims tried to give him sand, didn't they? How can you give a man like Martin Luther King sand? Why, he did something *I* wouldn't do! I wouldn't face those people down there, would you? The Muslims ain't going down there. They a money organisation. Muhammad's using my sons and he's using the black people, getting their money. You know what I'm talking about. He's got two mansions, boy!'

Cassius Sr, with his penchant for absolute statements, can satisfy himself that Elijah Muhammad is simply a money man working a grandiose con game on the American Negro, but a psychiatrist might take a different view of 'The Messenger of Allah'. Elijah said he was visited in the 1930s by a man named Wallace D. Fard, who turned out to be Allah, 'not a spook God', said Elijah, 'but a man.' Fard stayed with Mr and Mrs Elijah Muhammad, then known as Mr and Mrs Elijah Poole, for nearly four years and never went to sleep. Elijah was fond of telling how he would spy on Allah through the keyhole and 'Master Fard', without looking, would say, 'Why don't you come in?'

Elijah learned from Fard that whites were descended from monkeys and that they were created about 4,000 B.C. by Mr Yakub, a biologist who came to be known as 'the big head scientist' because he had been born with 'an unusual size head'. Yakub had been dabbling in evil experiments in his hometown of Mecca, according to Elijah Muhammad, and along with his sixty thousand followers was deported to an island in the Aegean, where he bred the white race. Elijah learned all this history from Master Wallace Fard. 'I am the one that the world has been expecting for the past two thousand years,' Fard told Elijah. 'My name is Mahdi; I am God; I came to guide you into the right path that you may be successful and see the hereafter.'

Such lessons in theology were restricted to the insides of the various Muslim 'mosques' in Negro ghettos of Detroit and Chicago and Miami and other cities until Cassius came along and began trumpeting them to any reporter who would listen. A day before his fight with Floyd Patterson, Clay shocked the gentlemen of the press by quoting from Elijah's book, *Message to the Blackman*, about the Mother of Planes, that Negro-manned, bomb-laden satellite described by Elijah Muhammad. Cassius added in a respectful tone of voice: 'On a clear night when you can see all the stars, look for the brightest. Watch it for a while. You'll see it shaking, that high up. Little white objects jump off it, make a circle, come back. Those are the bombers. On them are black men who never smile . . . '

Said Lawyer Gordon Davidson, 'The father didn't even know about the Muslims when he was putting all his ideas into Clay's head. But the great portion of the Muslim philosophy is shared by the great majority of Negroes, sixty per cent anyway. Things like the desire to have pride in their race, the idea that they're black men and not just ex-slaves and Negroes. And when the father talked about things like this he created the base for Cassius to do something he never could foresee. The irony is fantastic. The father spouting all of this ancestral background and blah-blah. All the Muslims needed was to capitalise on it and they did. Very ironic!'

'And now Cassius' father says he hates the Muslims,' said the fighter's Aunt Mary Clay Turner, 'but if he'd have hated 'em at first, he coulda led Cassius right out. Instead, the father kept on trying to lead Cassius and me and everybody else right into that kind of thinking. He leaned toward Muslim thinking, even though he never would try to be one himself.'

'The father set up the boy,' said one of the original Louisville Eleven, the businessmen who backed the young boxer. 'From the very beginning when we were dealing with the father a lot, when Cassius was still a minor, his father'd make statements that would be identical with those in *Muhammad Speaks*, the Muslim newspaper. In one of those early sessions, I think it was 1960, the father said to me, "We're not Negro, we're Arabs!" And when the money was divided up after each fight, he'd say things like, "See, Cassius? I told you you'd never get a break from a white man in Kentucky!"

Now the monster he created in this boy comes back to haunt him.'

Early in 1964, before Clay won the championship, his father began to realise what was happening to his sons Cassius and Rudolph, and immediately he issued a blast against the Muslims. 'They have been hammering at him and brainwashing him ever since he was eighteen. He's so confused he doesn't even know where he's at. They've ruined my two boys. They should run those Black Muslims out of the country before they ruin other fine young people . . . The Muslims taught my boys to hate white people, to hate women, to hate their mother.' It especially galled the father that he would get collect calls from 'Rudolph X'. 'I don't know no Rudolph X,' he would tell the operator, and refuse to accept charges. Later his sons became Rahman Ali and Muhammad Ali, but the father did not know them under those names, either.

According to Muhammad Ali himself, he first heard the truth and saw the light at a Muslim meeting in Miami or New York or Chicago when he was eighteen. Not that Christianity had any too strong a hold on him at the time. Those who listened closely to his early pronouncements about religion might have detected that potentially he was a backslider, as children of dogmatic religionists so often are. As a teenager, his attitude about Heaven and Hell, for example, was revealing. 'Last Sunday some cats I know said, "Cassius, Cassius, come on now and let's go to church; otherwise you won't get to Heaven," ' he said. ' "Hold on a minute," I said to them, "and let me tell you something else. When I've got me a hundred-thousand-dollar house, another quarter million stuck in the bank and the world title latched on to my name, then I'll *be* in Heaven. Walking around making twenty-five dollars a week, with four children crying at home 'cause they're hungry, *that's* my idea of Hell." I ain't studying about either one of them catching up with me in the graveyard.'

Cassius has given three different versions of his first indoctrination into Islamism, and the sceptic might be tempted to discard them all and go back to a statement made by Aunt Mary: 'He was brainwashed just like the Communists worked on our turncoats, and it started a long time ago, when he was sixteen. He came back from the Golden Gloves in Chicago and he had a Black Muslim phonograph record with him, and he used to play it over and over and over and over and over again. And sometimes I'd believe they'd hypnotised him. They had that boy hypnotised. He'd look at you funny, and I'd say to myself, "They musta fed him something before he came back this way!" '

Cassius told one reporter early in his pro career: 'I was at the corner of 125th Street and Lenox Avenue when I first heard the message. I didn't know who that Muslim speaker was, but everything he said made sense. The man made me think about many things I had wondered about. But I didn't join right away. I went to CORE, Urban League and NAACP meetings. I studied the Catholics, the Jehovah's Witnesses, Seventh-day Adventists, Baptists and Methodists in a search for knowledge. The most concrete thing I found in churches was segregation. Well, now I have learned to accept my own and be myself. I know we are original man and that we are the greatest people on the planet earth and our women the queens thereof.'

Later Cassius told me: 'My first contact with Islam was in Miami, Florida, about 1960 or early 1961. One of the brothers invited me to a meeting and I heard the truth and the facts about life and history and right away it hit me. It is not true that Malcolm X converted me when he visited me in Miami. It was the truth, the word itself, that converted me, what I heard when I first walked

Cassius singing with the late Sam Cooke

(*Photo: Tony Triolo*)

A champion's smile

into that meeting in Miami. I heard the minister saying, "Why are we called Negroes? Chinese are named after Chinamen, Cubans are named after Cubans, Indians are named after Indians . . . !' Cassius kept the list going for about two minutes, or one minute and fifty-five seconds longer than required to make his point. His habit of sticking on a list like a broken record passes for erudition in his intimate circles. ' "Hawaiians are named after Hawaiians," ' he went on, quoting the preacher. ' "Germans are named after Germans. Australians . . . Mexicans . . . Egyptians . . . Italians . . . Puerto Ricans . . . Indonesians . . . " ' Then he paused for emphasis, like his father, and loudly quoted the preacher's punchline: ' "BUT WHAT COUNTRY'S NAMED AFTER NEGROES?" ' Another pause. 'And I said to myself, "That's something to think about." '

And still later he told me, 'The first meeting I went to was in Chicago. All the writers heard I was going and they went there to catch me, in a Muslim Temple in South Chicago. Inside I saw nothing but six hundred, seven hundred people, all the women in their white robes, just like Mary in all the pictures with Jesus. Men all had on dark suits and bow ties and white shirts, neat haircuts. And I said, "Why all these FBI men and newsmen out here?" Then I stopped to think. Hell, I'm supposed to be free. I'm not downtown integrating and marching. I'm not trying to marry a white woman or cause race trouble or running white people out of their suburbs. I'm in my own neighbourhood. I'm not smoking. I'm not drinking. Everybody in here's praying. There's no winking, no flirting, no adultery. I said, "What's wrong, this must be right, this must be the real programme of God." So I went to the door and I called out, "Yeh, I'm here! Why?"

'They said, "Are you a Muslim?" and I said, "No, I'm not, not now. But the way you keep pressing me I just might be." I said, "They're the cleanest people next to God." And later on I met Elijah Muhammad. He's the Messenger of God. You won't see no power on earth no greater. *The Messenger of Allah.* If he tells me to do something, I do it, real fast, before he gets it out of his mouth. And when I found out his programme, that we're not Negroes, we're Asiatic black people, gods of the universe and fathers of all civilisation, and the queen of the planet earth, I knew truth when I heard it. I said, "That's God's truth, that's what I been looking for." '

As long ago as 1962 the Louisville Sponsoring Group was aware that the Black Muslims were romancing Clay, but the group's position was that religious matters were private. 'One of our first inklings came from the Louisville chapter of the NAACP,' said a spokesman. 'Clay had made some public statements about protest demonstrations to the effect that he didn't want dogs biting him, he wasn't a politician, things like that. The NAACP here had asked him to do some things that he turned down. And he told them, "I don't go where I'm not wanted." The NAACP didn't like the sound of this and they called us and met with us. And they said they'd found out the boy apparently was running with Black Muslims. We'd already begun to suspect. Rudy was converted before Cassius, and he'd sit at our meetings with his arms folded, eyes looking straight ahead, and he'd never say a word. We knew something was going on.'

The official announcement of Clay's conversion to Islam came three days after he defeated Sonny Liston in Miami Beach to become world heavyweight champion. 'A rooster crows only when it sees the light,' said Cassius at a press conference February 27, 1964. 'Put him in the dark and he'll never crow. I have seen the light and I'm crowing.' He had not intended to crow, but a reporter told him that Elijah Muhammad had let the news out at a meeting in Chicago. 'That is true, and I am proud of it,' Clay said. 'But what's all the commotion about? Nobody asks other people about their religion. But now I am the champion, I am the king; so it seems the world is all shook up about what I believe. You call it Black Muslims. I don't. This is a press word. It is not a legitimate name. Islam is a religion and there are seven hundred and fifty million people all over the world who believe in it, and I am one of them. Islam means peace. Yet people brand us as a hate group. They say we want to take over the country. They say we're Communists. That is not true. Followers of Allah are the sweetest people in the world. They don't carry knives. They don't tote weapons. They pray five times a day. The women wear dresses that come all the way to the floor and they don't commit adultery. The men don't marry white women. All they want to do is live in peace with the world. They don't hate anybody. They don't want to stir up any kind of trouble. All the meetings are held in secret, without any fuss or hate-mongering.'

Cassius raved on and on about his new religion, and hundreds of newspapers, including *The New York Times*, quoted him at length the next day, as though they were quoting a world-renowned theologian. 'Elijah Muhammad never had it so good,' said one of Clay's annoyed stablemates. 'Here he's been trying to peddle that screwy religion of his and getting no place, which is where he belongs, and then along comes this simple-minded kid falling for all the baloney and getting the Muslims the kind of publicity you couldn't buy. No wonder they broke their neck to get Cassius.'

'I get telephone calls every day,' the newspaper stories quoted the champion. 'They want to me carry signs. They want me to picket. They tell me it would be a wonderful thing if I married a white woman because this would be good for brotherhood. I don't want to be blown up. I don't want to be washed down sewers. I just want to be happy with my own kind.' He launched into his well-worn separation speech: 'Animals in the jungle flock together. Mexicans, Puerto Ricans, Chinese and Japanese all live better if they are together. I don't like hot Mexican food and I would be unhappy if somebody made me eat it. At the same time, you may not like what I like – turnip greens and hominy grits or country music. If you don't like it you shouldn't have to accept it.'

Clay finished with a personal vote of confidence in himself. 'I am a good boy,' he said. 'I never have done anything wrong. I have never been in jail. I have never been in court. I don't join any integration marches. I don't pay any attention to all those white women who wink at me. I don't carry signs. I don't impose myself on people who don't want me. If I go in somebody's house where I'm not welcome, I am uncomfortable. So I stay away. I like white people. I like my own people. They can live together in peace.'

Later he said: 'I used to be confused like most American black men. I used to want to be anything but black. I'd smoke once in a while, take a beer, pour whisky in my Coke and I was about to try out reefers when I listened to our leader, the Honourable Elijah Muhammad, that itty-bitty man.'

Odessa Grady Clay had the friendliest feelings toward the eleven wealthy men of the Louisville Sponsoring Group, but she charged them with one error of judgment when they failed to shield Cassius from the Muslims. 'The big mistake was when they sent him to train at Miami all by himself,' said Mrs Clay. 'That's when the Muslims got him. That's how Sam Saxon got him and talked that Muslim stuff to him every day. 'Cause I went there one year with Cassius and this old Sam, the Muslim man, was in Cassius's room every night, brainwashing him. If somebody'd been with Cassius, they'd never have got to him.'

Later a variant of Mrs Clay's theory was worked up by Joe Louis, the former heavyweight champion, who travelled briefly with Cassius before quitting with the announcement, 'I was born a Baptist and I'll die a Baptist.' Said Louis: 'He got off on the wrong foot. He got no help from his Louisville management. They stayed on one side of town and him on the other. He ran wild. Nobody told him to talk to people. Now nobody can stop him.'

To the impartial observer of Clay's history, it is difficult to see how any measure short of house arrest could have kept the young fighter out of the Black Muslim movement. The religion did not have to seek out the man. Christianity, with its preachments of loving neighbours and the brotherhood of mankind, could not satisfy a mystical, unsettled Negro youth who was weaned on stories about lynching and rape and the lying, deceitful white man, plus the moon and the stars and the flickering mysteries of the East. 'He was an absolutely perfect prospect for the Black Muslims,' said William Faversham, the member of the group who was closest to Clay during the early professional years. 'He's a boy for whom this sort of Alice-in-Wonderland religion would hold an appeal. He's a mystic himself. The universe fascinates him. Early in the game he used to have visions. He likes that sort of thing.'

One can imagine how the Black Muslim penchant for prognostication must have hit the ears of the young Clay, who had lived on prophecies for years ('I will be the world's heavyweight champion') and who was the son of a man who lived on prophecies ('And I'll have a factory called Clay's Enterprises and I'll employ all my relatives').

'You have to understand the role of prophecy,' explained a Louisville schoolteacher, himself a Negro. 'If you can't stand the world you live in, and you can't change it, you've got to believe in magic, in predictions. That's Cassius when he was growing up, living with that wild father and all that crazy talk around the house. You've got to believe that things are gonna change. So predictions have a great charm and appeal. "Next year the white man's gonna lose his power." "1966'll be a bad year for the white man." That's great news to some people dumb enough to believe it. Believing in predictions is a way of warding off evil in the present when you can't ward it off any other way. You can bear living miserable if you believe a prediction that tomorrow will be better. That's why you get so much predicting and prophecy in the Negro churches. That's why you get so much predicting and prophecy from Cassius Clay, too.'

Clay himself analysed the phenomenon of forecasting the future. 'What do all these people sitting there in Madison Square Garden think?' he once told a reporter. 'They ask, "Can I do it again?" They want to know. They want to see that *round*. People are superstitious. It's the *round* that gets them. They don't come to see me win. They come to see that *round*. People run to priests. They pray and shout in church. People is spooky-minded. They look at the moon. They wonder about numbers. Preachers say Jesus called them but they got no proof. I got proof. The round I call is the round they must fall.'

A reporter once dared Clay to predict a knock-out to the very second. 'Seconds are gimmick talk,' Cassius said angrily. 'There's nothing spooky or ghostly about calling the round – it's all science. I go into a conference with myself and then I prophesy. You start with the thought and then you turn it into reality, like the scientist figured out how to make the jet before he built it.'

Later Clay's former assistant trainer, Drew 'Bundini' Brown, said, 'When I first met the champ, I told him he was a phony, doing all that predicting. He said to me,

"Every time I call the round, I'm scared to death." There were tears in both of our eyes.'

Young Clay was always obsessed by prophecy, and Elijah Muhammad did not fail to satisfy his appetite. 'Look what he say here,' Cassius told me one morning, pointing to a chapter title in *Message to the Blackman*: AMERICA IS FALLING HER DOOM IS SEALED. 'And he teaches that before the year's over all Negroes in America are gonna be Muslims, before 1966 is over,' Clay went on. 'And he is teaching that this year all Negroes will rise into the knowledge of the truth, and he don't hide it. And the press can tell by the end of the year if he was right. And he says that things are getting close to the fulfilment of the Bible, where the Bible says you can tell when the end of time is coming because there will be wars and rumours of wars, men flying like a bird, horseless carriages, buildings being teared down like mad, daughters against mothers and mothers against daughters, men taking the place of women . . . '

'See, I read my Bible,' the fighter's father had told me a few days earlier, 'and we right on the time for Judgment Day now. Saint John asked God how will we know when it's the time, and God said people will be riding horseless carriages, people'll be flying like birds, and man will be loving man, and there'll be more tearing down and destroying and building up than ever before. Am I right? Ummmmmmmmmmm. God said when the time comes there'll be wars and rumours of wars. Are they that? Ummmmmmmmmmm. God's gonna come down and the devil's gonna try to tackle him, but God's gonna destroy the devil, take the key away from him and lock him up. And then God'll come down and rise nothing but the Christians! People like Elijah Muhammad's people, they will not be in the first resurrection. They're false prophets. God says beware of false prophets who come to you dressed as sheep but are raging wolves beneath.'

159

'The old man is something else,' said a family friend. 'He sits there quoting the Bible and attacking the Black Muslims and if you listen closely you can hardly tell 'em apart!'

After relations with Cassius the elder had come almost to an end, young Cassius installed Elijah Muhammad in a parental role in his life, and sometimes in a supernatural role. 'Look at the nation today,' Cassius said. 'The sit-ins didn't work; the swim-ins didn't work, the walk-ins, roll-ins, none of 'em worked. Thirty, forty was shot down in Los Angeles like animals, children who had mothers who were crying; children who wanted to live and breathe the fresh air God gave 'em are now daid and in the grave just because they were trying to get justice. So there's nothing for the nation but destruction. God himself must come, and he's here! *Elijah Muhammad is the man to fill the need*. If you don't believe it, just listen to what he says and watch it.'

And yet Clay's subservience to the god-like leader, like most of his personality traits, appears to be part real and part pretence or self-delusion. One afternoon he told me how the wispy little Muhammad, like an angry father, had taken his driver's licence away. 'Muhammad ain't playing, man!' Cassius said. 'He makes you live clean and righteous. When he catch you, boy, you caught! I can't drive no more. I got to have a driver. I had that police trouble about my driving, those tickets, and Muhammad say he don't want to read about me in no more trouble; so he said, "You just quit driving!" and I had to quit. He's *that* powerful! Anything he say, we do, man! The whole country's scared of him, they don't even bother him.' Cassius forgot that he had arrived at our rendezvous minutes before behind the wheel of his big black Cadillac. The Muslim hierarchy is indulgent toward the champion in such matters, and in general treats him like a rich old uncle with a heart condition.

Thus he is not punished for occasional violations of Elijah's specific orders, and for eating more than once a day, and for minor offences which might get another member of the sect suspended for as long as five years, as was one of Cassius's friends ('for getting caught with a woman, you know what I mean, man,' Clay explained).

The champion may buddy up to one or another of Elijah's trusted lieutenants, but his ultimate allegiance is to the big boss and to the philosophy the big boss has spelled out in the three decades since Allah appeared to him. Anyone who fell out with Muhammad fell out with Cassius, as the late Malcolm X, once a close friend of Cassius, quickly learned. Malcolm broke with Muhammad over some of the leader's personal habits, and immediately Malcolm found that Cassius was no longer his best disciple. The last word between them was a message to Cassius on his arrival in Ghana for a triumphant swing through Africa. 'Because a billion of our people in Africa, Arabia and Asia love you blindly,' Malcolm wired, 'you must now be forever aware of your tremendous responsibilities to them. You must never say or do anything that will permit your enemies to distort the beautiful image you have here among our people.'

Holding the wire in his hand, Clay told Herbert Muhammad, the leader's son, that he had seen Malcolm in his robes the day before 'and he didn't look very responsible to me.' Said Cassius: 'Man, did you get a look at him? Dressed in that funny white robe and wearing a beard and walking with that cane that looked like a prophet's stick? Man, he's gone! He's gone so far out he's out completely. Doesn't that just go to show, Herbert, that Elijah is the most powerful? Nobody listens to that Malcolm any more.'

When a Muslim terror squad assassinated Malcolm in front of hundreds of witnesses, Cassius said: 'Malcolm X was my friend and he was the friend of everybody *as long as he was a member of Islam.* Now I don't want to talk about him. All of us were shocked at the way he was killed. Elijah Muhammad has denied that the Muslims were responsible. We are not a violent people. We don't carry guns.' When it was established later that Muslims had undeniably perpetrated the murder, Cassius refused to discuss Malcolm X any further.

Another of Clay's close friends was beaten up by Black Muslims in Boston, and again Cassius immediately showed where his fealty lay. 'He's nothing to me,' he said. 'He was welcome as a friend as long as he was a registered Muslim. But not any more . . . ' The friend had recommended that Clay quit the Muslims because he might be roughed up himself, to which the champion replied: 'I will never leave the Muslims. If it weren't for the Muslims, I'd be nothing.'

Despite a certain air of capriciousness, which creeps into almost everything Clay does, he seems to be in earnest about his religion. Asking him the simplest question about the Nation of Islam can be an exhausting process unless one has time on one's hands. On a television discussion programme, someone made the mistake of asking Clay the significance of the name Muhammad Ali. The answer was in perfect Stengelese: 'Our religious leader the Muslims of the believers in the religion of Islam here in America – that's taught by Elijah Muhammad – honourable Elijah Muhammad – he named this great, honourable name – Muhammad Ali – after my victory over Liston. And I would like to explain to you that he teaches us that many people – that is a good question you asked – he teaches us that most people, all people from certain countries have names that have meanings. Like Mr Cassius Marcellus Clay was a slave fighter, the white man – I should say Caucasian. Way back they used to write about this, way back even before I joined the Islamic religion and got my name changed.

They used to talk about this great man named Cassius Clay who was a white. Now he named my great-great-grand-daddy after him. Which means that this was not the name of a black man, but the name of a white man. And like for an example if I told you here comes Mr Chang Chong you would picture a yellow man from China. If I told you here come Mr Krushchev, you would picture a Russian. If I say here come Mr Castro, you would picture a Cuban. If I say here come Mr Lumumba or Mr Nkrumah or Kenyatta, Africans, right? Here come Mr White Cloud, Morning Trees, Tall Star or Silver Moon, you would picture Indians. But if I said here come Mr Smith, Mr Robinson, Mr Clay, Mr Tree, Mr Fish, Mr Bird, you would not know what colour he is until you saw him. He could be Negro or white because the people put at two million Negroes as the Honourable Elijah Muhammad teaches us here are named after the masters when we were freed a hundred years ago. But we were not given our names back. So therefore we who follow the honourable Elijah Muhammad it is indeed an honour for him to give us a name such as Muhammad Ali and the name Muhammad means one who is worthy of praises and one who is praiseworthy. And Ali means the most high. Clay only meant dirt with no ingredients.'

While Cassius paused for air, somebody said, 'It would be awful nice if one of these days the people who are white quit being so proud of being white and the people who are black quit being so proud of being black and maybe it would be better if we all had names like tree and bush and things like that.'

Said Cassius: 'Men should not be named after fishes; man should not be named after horses; man should not be named after birds and trees and woods and man should be named, men are supreme over all animals and he look like he kind of silly naming himself after a horse. Man is the most high. So Ali means the most high.

Muhammad means worthy of praises and praiseworthy. So I think I have two names that really just stand up and hold its own against anyone on the planet earth.'

A few minutes later he was launched on a sales talk about his leader: 'I want to be a Muslim because after seeing the teachings that the honourable Elijah Muhammad is teaching these so-called Negroes in America, the onliest man who has black people sticking together, not begging, not on their hands and knees, forcing themselves on people that don't want him. He's the onliest man that have following teaching the so-called Negroes unity among their own, mainly respect of the black woman which he has never gotten from four hundred years out of black men. He is the onliest man teaching us the knowledge of our true language. This is Arabic. He is the onliest man teaching us the knowledge of our history, our culture, names and our true God whose proper name is Allah before we were brought to the shores of North America. He's the onliest man who is connecting us with all of the people in Africa, Asia, Egypt, Arabia, Sudan, Indonesia, Pakistan, who has never recognised American Negroes, and he is the onliest man who have followers that the white Americans really respect.'

Cassius professes to believe without reservation in Muhammad, even in the outermost reaches of the leader's message. To Clay, the dietary prohibitions of the Islamic religion, as spelled out by Elijah Muhammad, have the force of divine law (even though he sometimes honours them in the breach), and he speaks of food restrictions like a Christian reciting a Sunday School lesson. 'Our beans are crushed and mashed and cooked. We eat only whole wheat bread and whole wheat muffins. Cabbages and greens and green beans are cooked without fattenings and pork. We don't eat any sweet potatoes because they're not good for the digestive system. We eat squash cooked like sweet potatoes. We don't eat lima beans and collard greens; these are hard, animal foods. We don't eat shrimp, catfish, crabs, lobsters, all swine of the sea, and we don't eat garbage eaters like the hog on the land and the buzzard in the sky. We have a knowledge of these things, and once we start eating Egyptian cooked rice and Arabian baked string beans, carrot pies, squash pies, buttermilk pies, we're not at home with what you whites eat.'

He was asked how it happens that some of the Black Muslims' dietary rules conflict with those of the world's 750 million Moslems, to whom the Black Muslims claim a spiritual kinship. 'Well, Allah taught our leader more than he taught those African Moslems,' Clay explained. 'The African Moslems aren't as wise as us. The proof is all the African leaders have white wives, or a lot of 'em do. They're not as wise as us.'

Like a child who learned his catechism, Cassius has all the answers. Do the Muslims teach hate? 'In a way, we do. But are we wrong to hate the murders and the unjust treatment that we're getting? Sure, we hate that. But we're righteous people. We rely on Allah, and we don't bother nobody.' What about Elijah Muhammad's constant refrain that all white men are devils? 'Elijah Muhammad teaches us that he didn't know about that hisself till thirty-five, forty years ago when God, in the person of Master Wallace Fard, came to America and he, Allah in the person of Master Wallace Fard, taught Elijah Muhammad. And Elijah Muhammad teaches us that this is not his own, it's just the truth that God taught him. And if God taught him that all white men are devils, and we believe that Muhammad is from God, then we have to believe it. And no white man has ever yet in the thirty-five years of Muhammad's teaching, no white man have took Elijah Muhammad to court about it. No white man has stood up and debated or challenged him to prove they wasn't devils, or invited him to a duel or a discussion, or fined him. Not one white man in America has stood up and said, "We are not devils, prove it, what's this false charge?" And this teaching is now all over America.'

Until the religious issue all but severed relations between them, the Clays, Junior and Senior, used to engage in wild arguments about such matters. 'The Muslims know I could bring him back to the church,' the father said with sublime faith in his own rhetoric, ' 'cause I drilled him all the time. I drilled him hard!'

There were long debates when young Cassius accepted his new name of Muhammad Ali. 'Cassius Marcellus Clay was the most beautiful name,' said Odessa, as though the name were now dead and buried. 'It was from the Romans. It was a warrior's name.'

Another who argued with young Clay was his plain-spoken 'auntie', Mary Clay Turner. 'He'd pick certain things out of the Bible to prove his points,' Aunt Mary recalled, 'and I'd say to him, "Well, why don't you read something else in this good book besides those things you have underlined? You read on this page and then you flip ahead fifty pages for your next point and then maybe a hundred more and you point to something else." I said, "Read the whole thing! Don't let nobody dictate to you and tell you what to read!"

'If Cassius had been reading like I been reading he wouldn't have been caught in that Muslim mess,' Aunt Mary went on. 'Right now if a man comes up to my boys and tells 'em to sign their name with an X, like a Muslim, my boys'll tell 'em, "Why, that's the way my oldest great-grandmother was taught to write, sign her name with an X to keep from learning how to write," I been over these things with Cassius so often, but now I give up. I don't even say nothing any more. Why, you have to be almost totally illiterate to be sold that Muslim bill of goods! I'll just plain old give you the facts. *You have to be illiterate!* Cassius is about the cleanest thing in the whole confounded Muslim organisation. All the rest of them have scars and smears on their names. If they haven't once been hustlers, well, they're hustling now! If they haven't been robbers, they're robbing now! This is it, you know I'm not lying! Practically every one of 'em's been in prison. Cassius falls for all that business about no drinking and no smoking, but he didn't know they drink behind the doors, and cuss, and whip their mamas and do everything. And they'd kill you just as quick as they'd kill me, and don't you forget it!'

Aunt Mary talks like someone who has abandoned all hope for her nephew, but Cassius Sr, with his perpetual ebullience, still grasps for straws. 'I just can't believe Cassius hates white people. It's not in his blood to be like that. We might bring him back. Lemme explain something to you. Ummmmmmmmmmm. Suppose you're going from here to 12th and Broadway. You don't know how to get there and you ask somebody and he points the opposite way of the right way, and you start off. Now you can only go so far till you come to Florida and the ocean when you're looking for 12th and Broadway. Right? And you turn around and get on the right road. Ummmmmmmmm. That's deep, isn't it? You might think you hate, you might be taught to hate, but you don't *really* hate. You know why? Now hold on now! Because you a man, and I'm a man, and we both from God. We all have one father: God in Heaven. And the world's founded on love, and man was saved on love, and redeemed on love. Ummmmmmmmm. How long was Cassius here the other day, Peaches?'

'About twenty-five minutes,' Mrs Clay answered.

'They keep him away from me,' the father said. 'They know I could bring him back. They tell him he can't stay around his parents.'

'They don't like me 'cause I'm light-skinned,' the mother said. 'I can't help what I am. They hard on me. Yeh, they *hard* on me.'

'Yeh,' said Cassius the elder. 'They hard on all of us.'

Certainly the Muslims were hard on Sonji Roi, the beautiful Chicago entertainer who married Clay with the blessings of the Muslims and lost him to their insistent pressure on her husband. 'They've stolen my man's mind,' Sonji said when Cassius filed for divorce. But as in so many other matters, Clay's attitude toward women was distorted long before the Muslim influence came into his life. Just as the religion did not have to seek out the man, so the religion did not have to mould the man's attitude toward women, which seems to be that they are an inferior type of human: sinful, evil and temptingly corrupt. 'When he was real small,' Odessa Grady Clay said in a revealing memory about her older son, 'he loved to chase chickens and dogs. When we took him out to his uncle's in the country the first thing he would do would be chase the chickens and ducks. And when he grew up you know what he used to do when he come home from grade school? He always liked to run girls with switches! We'd say, "You don't run pretty girls!" He was always chasing girls, when he was eight, nine, ten years old. Every day after school he did it.' She began to laugh almost hysterically. 'And he always would bring me flowers when he was real small. Oh, he is such a kind-hearted, sympathetic person, just as good as gold!'

Later, in the middle of a lengthy interview, I suddenly asked Cassius: 'Why did you used to chase girls with switches?'

After a long pause, he said, ' 'Cause they was always wrong and they needed a whuppin'.'

On one level or another of his thinking, Cassius

168

appears to have made the decision to handle the woman problem by staying away from them. He treats them with elaborate courtesy, but steers clear of any personal relationships. When he was on one of his trips, the Clay bus stopped in Fredericksburg, Va., and six young and pretty Negro girls rushed up to talk to the champion. When one asked for a souvenir, Cassius said, 'I'd give you my shirt, but I can't get out a fresh one. Lord knows I need one.'

One of the passionate young men in Clay's party jumped up and said, 'That's all right. Take mine, sweet thing!'

'Hush!' Clay said. 'These little foxes wants to talk to the champ.' After a polite conversation, he escorted them out of the bus and bade them a courteous farewell. 'O . . . OOO,' he said when the girls were gone. 'Sometimes it's *so* hard to be righteous.'

'This you can quote,' said Solomon McTier, one of Clay's handlers. 'He lives clean. He waves at the girls and keep right on walking!'

'I've never seen anybody train or keep his body in shape the way this man does, and it's hard to understand,' said another member of Clay's camp. 'Here he is a beautiful fighter, a beautiful human being, and at the age of twenty-four years old, he renews himself with the women like a man of sixty. Why, after he won the title against Liston, Sam Cooke, you remember Sam, the singer? Sam Cooke had three beautiful young ladies come over to Cassius's house in Miami. And these three women grabbed the heavyweight champion of the world and they said we're gonna go out and celebrate. But he would not go out and celebrate. At exactly quarter to one he told the three girls, "I'm sorry, ladies, you are gonna have to leave. I'm gonna go to bed." Now can you imagine that? Whether he was tired or not, here's a fellow that's just won the championship of the world, made his dreams come true, and he isn't gonna have some fun with these ladies? A young beautiful guy like this? And a very normal guy at that? You figure a guy like this is gonna go somewhere and get lost with the chicks after training so hard and sacrificing so hard to get the title. And at this very moment I can't understand it. I still see girls call this guy and want to come over and he'll say, "I'm sorry, I got to get my rest." '

Before Sonji came along, Cassius engaged in a few minor flirtations, but for the most part all his normal desires appeared to be sublimated into boxing. 'He did have a crush on Wilma Rudolph, the Olympic sprinter,' said Clarence 'Slick' Royalty, a prominent sports figure from Louisville, 'but nothing came of it. When she was here, Cassius was trying to hold her hand all the time, but she wasn't interested in him at all. Every time she'd get up to go some place he'd jump up beside her and hold her hand, but she wouldn't respond. She finally went back to Tennessee A&I and got married, and I think it bothered Cassius a little bit.' Later he was linked romantically with a Sudanese girl named Rechima, whom he met on his trip to Africa. 'She wears this wrap-around dress and has a gem in her forehead,' Clay told reporters. 'And she's beautiful just like me.' But after a few months of separation, he stopped talking about her, and later denied that he had ever thought of Rechima as anything but a friend.

And suddenly Cassius was married. To the amazement of his friends and to the complete surprise of his biographers of the press, Clay drove to Gary, Indiana with Sonji Roi and was married in a closely guarded civil ceremony. After the wedding, he submitted to a short press conference. He said Sonji was twenty-two, a model and editor on various magazines, a Muslim like himself, and a woman who would fade into the background and keep her mouth shut, like a good Muslim wife. He said he and Sonji would go to Egypt and 'when my children are born they won't be born in America. They'll be born in the hereafter.'

He was asked where the hereafter was. 'Somewhere near Arabia,' said Cassius. He added that the 'wicked world' was on the verge of being destroyed; 'the way things are shaping up it won't be but about ten years.' He said he and Sonji were not members of the wicked race; they were both 'Asiatic'.

Sonji Roi was not, in fact, the twenty-two-year-old editor of various magazines but the twenty-seven-year-old once-married mother of one child. For five years she had worked as barmaid at the Archway Supper Club on Chicago's South Side, and during that time she had been the girl friend of various star Negro athletes. Then Herbert Muhammad, the rotund son of 'The Messenger of Allah', spotted her and put her to work in the office of his newspaper, *Muhammad Speaks*. Before her first week was over, Sonji met Cassius and struck sparks. 'You never saw two people fall for each other so fast in your life,' said a Clay confidante. 'It was *bang!* Just like the movies.' Sonji was regarded as an odd choice by some of the people around Cassius. 'You figure it out,' said Dr Pacheco. 'Here is a man who spends all his time talking about women who paint their faces, women who drink, and what the hell does he fall for? A woman who paints her face, wears short dresses, drinks and smokes. Is that childish innocence on his part, or is there a little Elmer Gantry in him? I tell you: behind this superguy, there are many contradictions!'

Clay's own version of the affair with Sonji had them meeting on July 3, 1964, and beginning a common-law marriage three weeks later in Miami. 'I said I would like to take her with me and would she marry me? This was in Miami. "Would you marry me common-law to justify our driving to Los Angeles and checking into hotels on the way out and checking in the largest, biggest hotel in Los Angeles as my wife and taking you to religious meetings as my wife? I cannot be seen to commit adultery. It just cannot be in my name. I am the heavyweight champion of the world. You must marry as common-law to travel with me and check in hotels with me." She did marry me common-law. That justified my sleeping with her in the bed and cohabit with her all the way on my trip to Los Angeles and back to Chicago.'

According to Cassius, Sonji also agreed to become a Muslim. 'That was the onliest reason I married her, because she agreed to do everything I wanted her to do.' She became a Muslim by writing a letter to National Secretary John Ali proclaiming her belief in the Nation of Islam and promising to register as a Muslim. 'Once that letter is accepted and you get lessons, you're a member,' Cassius explained. 'She was accepted even to the extent of teaching the girls and all of the ladies in Boston, Massachusetts, on her experiences and her life, at the time we were training, and she also had the honour of eating dinner with her leader twice with me. He accepted her as his daughter. He offered his home to show he accepted her . . . But I told her to be my wife she must wear her dresses at least three inches below her knees, she must take off lipstick, she must quit drinking and smoking in order to be seen with me, going to our religious meetings which was due to come up.'

After their civil marriage in Indiana, Cassius kept Sonji in almost complete isolation from the press. Reporters who approached her in training camp were sharply admonished by Cassius himself to stay away, 'if you ever want to have another interview with me.' Anyone who asked Sonji about the marriage received only a cold glance in reply. The pretty ex-barmaid was trying dutifully to live her role as a Muslim wife. One day Chris Dundee, brother of Angelo and a close friend of

Cassius, had a short conversation with Sonji in the Fifth Street Gym in Miami Beach. Chris talks with his hands, like the warm, friendly South Philadelphia Italian he is, and he has difficulty keeping them off whomever he is conversing with. To talk to Chris Dundee is to get your back slapped, your shoulders pommelled and your arms squeezed. After Chris spoke to Sonji, Cassius called him to one side and said, 'You know you're not supposed to touch a Muslim woman? Now I know you didn't mean no harm, but you got to remember. Don't touch any Muslim woman!'

Said Chris Dundee later: 'It gave me a creepy feeling to be talked to like that.'

Six months went by before Clay allowed a reporter to talk to Sonji, and then it was only a short interview. 'I kept her away from the press until I could coach her,' Cassius explained. 'Didn't want my baby to say the wrong things.' He explained that the Islamic religion called for women to remain in the background. 'It's pretty demanding,' said Sonji in her first meeting with the press. Behind the scenes, she was getting a neckful of the Islamic faith. 'They were on him night and day,' she said later. 'Pestering him, pestering him, never gave him a minute's peace.'

Occasionally the two would have a minor public spat, indicative of the smouldering resentment underneath. One day Cassius rushed into the house in Miami after training and poured himself a tall glass of orange juice. 'You ain't cooled off yet, and you already had two glasses of orange when you left the gym,' Sonji said.

'Who you, a fighter?' Cassius exclaimed hotly. 'You a fighter?' He swallowed the juice in one gulp.

A few months later Cassius asked a Miami court for an annulment. His suit complained: 'Prior to and at the time of the marriage and for the purpose of inducing plaintiff to consent to marriage she falsely and fraudulently represented and promised that on the pronouncement of the marital vows she would adopt the Islamic faith as her own and would without deviation adhere to its tenets and requirements, [but] she knew at the time the promises were false and fraudulent and secretly intended not to convert or adhere to these tenets. On June 11 an incident occurred when she told him she would not convert or adhere to the tenets and never intended to.'

Said Sonji: 'We've always had our little arguments about clothes. I told him that if I were embarrassing him I would stay out of the picture. I just want to be his wife and I won't let them take him away from me just like that.' She said she had tried to adhere to the rule of Muslimism, that she had quit drinking and smoking and ate only the foods prescribed by Elijah Muhammad.

At pre-trial hearings, Cassius testified that he was in training for his second fight with Sonny Liston when he realised that his wife did not intend to comply with the tenets of Islam. 'With all the world there, the Associated Press, the *Boston Globe*, African, Asian, European newspapers,' Clay said, 'she walked into the press conference with a blue jean, tight tight skin-tight blue jean suit on . . . This was about three or four days before my fight in Lewison, Maine, May 25, 1965 . . . Then after the fight in Maine we drove to Chicopee, Massachusetts, stayed there about a day and a half. She put on a short short short tight dress with no sleeves or nothing, contrary to everything that she had been wearing, and she walked into the lobby in this dress, went into the dining room in it, and I pulled her to the room and I asked her, "Why would you walk into the lobby around the world embarrassing me in these type sexual designed clothes showing all parts or many parts of your body?" and she says, "You have won your fight. I no longer have to pretend with you. I have never wanted to be a Muslim. I never will be a Muslim." Unquote. Excuse the expression, "To hell with all of you Muslims. You give me some money and I won't embarrass you in front of all these reporters, and I will catch a plane and will leave here and go to Chicago." '

Clay was asked if he had loved Sonji when he married her. 'I would like to say that I loved her only if she would follow me in my way of life and if she would take my name and everything else that I could give her and be what I wanted her to be. That's the onliest reason I would love her.'

When the case came to trial, it developed that Cassius had no genuine grounds for a divorce, beyond the testimony of one 'Samuel X. Saxon' to the effect that in his earshot Sonji had promised 'to comply with the Muslim faith.' Cap'n Sam was cast in a familiar role: seconding Cassius.

'Cassius had no real grounds at all,' said one of Sonji's advisors, 'so we just sat down and worked out a divorce. We asked him how much he'd pay to get out of the marriage and it developed he would pay a hundred and fifty thousand dollars to her and twenty-two thousand five hundred for legal fees. So that was the end of that.'

Slowly the wounds of the divorce healed, and Cassius began talking about getting married again. 'I have no one in mind,' he said one day, 'but I'll tell you this: the next time I marry it'll be a girl of seventeen or eighteen – one that I can raise to my way of thinking.'

Part Six

A WHITE MAN WHO HAD KNOWN CASSIUS CLAY FOR
several years visited the world heavyweight champion at
his Miami home and came away shaking his head
dolefully. 'I got there kinda late in the afternoon,' the
man said, 'and it looked like a lawn party was going on.
Clay was surrounded by little kids, eight or ten of 'em, all
Negroes, little children on his lap, little girls climbing
all over him, and he was nuzzling them and kissing
them: big sloppy kisses. And all around him were his
yes-men – his brother Rudy leading the pack and laughing
at everything he said. Cassius started a joke and Rudy
broke up at the first line and I asked him what he was
laughing about, the joke had just started, and Rudy
said, "Oh, I know this is gonna be *so* funny!" And Sam
Saxon was there giving Cassius that "Yes, suh, yes, suh."
And there were coloured men from downtown telling
him how he's the greatest fighter that ever lived, and
Clay agreeing for all he was worth. And it made you
wonder just how much approval, how much attention
does this boy need? It was like that movie, *The Great
Man*, except that the movie didn't have all those references
to that children's game called Black Muslims. Sitting
around talking about how they won't eat pork, shrimp;
how lobster's the swine of the sea. You go out there to
his place and you see all that and it's like being on a

pirate ship with an insane captain and a broken compass. And then you realise all of a sudden, "Holy Mother! That's where the heavyweight championship lives!" '

Whatever chance there might have been for Clay to return to the world of reality seems to be slipping quickly away. The last responsible man who had any control over him was Angelo Dundee, and even that faithful retainer has begun to make noises about dropping out. Every day Cassius pulls the constricting tentacles of Black Islam more tightly around him, permitting and even encouraging the Muslims to get him up in the morning and put him to bed at night. He goes through life like a man under voluntary house arrest. The valuable financial advice offered to him gratis by the businessmen of the Louisville Sponsoring Group is spurned. The excellent legal counselling offered by lawyers for the group is rejected in favour of 'personal' lawyers of the proper colour. The list of Muslim camp followers, paid out of Clay's own pocket, grows longer and longer. The result is that Clay is always verging on insolvency.

Oddly enough, young Cassius started his professional life under the direction of a group of men whose financial advice was not only sought but purchased in the public market at a premium. And these eleven men turned Cassius over to the best boxing brains available. Clay became heavyweight champion more or less in spite of the boxing advice handed out to him; his natural ability was such that he could argue with his mentors and ignore their admonitions and still become the best heavyweight boxer in the world. But by turning his back on the professional advice of his original eleven backers, he managed also to become the brokest heavyweight champion since Joe Louis. Said William Faversham, one of the original members of the group: 'The thing that's disturbed us terribly over the years is the fact that we were successful businessmen and we were at his service, and if Cassius had allowed us to help him with his investments he'd be well off today. Take W. L. Lyons Brown, the chairman of the board of our company, Brown Forman. Lyons is a very wealthy man and he's made his money out of this company. If you had bought the stock of Brown Forman in 1951 you'd have done better than if you'd have bought IBM at the same time. Then Lyons made another fortune in oil. And he's a typical member of this group behind Cassius. Take Archie Foster. He's now the president of Ted Bates Advertising. He also made a great amount of money in oil. We have another fellow who's made a great deal of money in real estate. We had all kinds of financial brains that could have helped Cassius, if he'd let them. But he'd just take his money and go. And the hell of it is his money didn't disappear in riotous living, either. In the early days he didn't spend a lot of money on himself outside of a couple of Cadillacs. I remember when he didn't have more than two suits of clothes. Of course, he was very generous with his relatives. At the outset, when we first signed the contract, he gave his mother and father ten thousand dollars. He said that was for raising him.'

The original contract with the Louisville Sponsoring Group specified a $10,000 bonus for signing, and all of that money was signed over to his parents by the eighteen-year-old boxer. Cassius knew there would be more, much more, where the $10,000 came from, and he was right. The contract called for a $4,000 no-strings guarantee for two years, training allowances that would have satisfied the tastes of Cleopatra, and fifty per cent of all earnings. Behind the money was a pool of $25,000, put up by the cream of Louisville's sporting society. Cassius confided to friends: 'All they want is to get their change back and a chance to impress their friends by saying, "That's my boy; after the fight I'll take you back to the dressing-room to meet the new champ." ' Perhaps so, but one has to admire the courage of the group. In those years, Cassius was just another promising young professional. To be sure, he had won the Olympic gold medal, as had the current champion, Floyd Patterson. But aside from Patterson, Olympic gold medal winners had proved disappointing as pros. And Clay's big mouth guaranteed an almost endless round of ragging by friends of the Louisville eleven at bridge parties and social functions. They had to become inured to such remarks as: 'What's your loudmouth had to say today?' and 'Can't you teach that fighter of yours some manners?' One member of the group said, with a note of hope and expectancy in his voice: 'We may find it exasperating, but not when we count the receipts.' And the group was performing a service to the city of Louisville: boxing, in those years, was under the shadow of Frankie Carbo and Blinky Palermo and other shady figures, and Cassius would be forever shielded from their influence.

'In Cassius,' said Bill Faversham, 'we saw a good local boy with a clean background from start to finish. With the proper help and encouragement, he could bring credit to himself and his hometown. There are plenty of wolves who would leap at the chance to get their paws on Cassius, to exploit him and then to drop him. We think we can bring him along slowly, get him good fights and make him the champion he wants to be.' Said another member of the group, also speaking the truth but getting at it from another point of the compass: 'Let me give you the official line. We are behind Cassius Clay to improve the breed of boxing, to do something nice for a deserving, well-behaved Louisville boy and, finally, to save him from the jaws of the hoodlum jackals. I don't know who composed that – maybe the executive committee – but I think it's beautiful. I think its fifty per cent true, but also fifty per cent hokum. What I want to do, like a few others, is to make a bundle of money. Why, do you know a Clay–Liston fight might gross a winner's share of three million? Split that up and it comes out one and a half million for Cassius and one and a half million for the syndicate. Best of all, it comes out a hundred and fifty thousand for me.'

The financial dreams of the sponsoring group and the financial dreams of its protégé never came true. The backers turned a profit, but after taxes it was hardly enough to pay them for the years of frustration and annoyance they had to endure with Cassius. With only a few exceptions the huge gates that could have rewarded their investments failed to materialise as Clay became less and less popular with the public, at the same time as his expenses soared. And Clay himself had little or nothing to show for his years at centre-stage. 'It's a funny thing,' said Dr Pacheco. 'He's made a hell of a lot of money, I mean take-home keepin' money. They figure he's had a hundred thousand dollars paid to him *after* taxes in the last couple of years, just as walking around money, free and clear. But Cassius thinks he's made a million, that he's worth a million. Then they show him he hasn't got a million in the bank. And all of a sudden it's come to him, this realisation that he doesn't have this money he's talking about. The million-dollars-a-fight days are over; he's not ever gonna make a million a fight. And he has nothing.'

'I tell him he's gonna be broke from all those leeches around him, but I tell him that so he *won't*,' said Cassius Sr. 'I drill him all the time. Cassius isn't gonna wind up broke. He's too smart for that. He'll go into some kind of business. But I have to keep telling him that he'll wind up broke to keep it from happening. You dig? Like I used to tell him when he was a little boy: there was this kid down the corner, much worser'n Cassius, and I'd say to Cassius, "Why can't you be good like that little boy there?" And I knew this Jerry, his name was, I knew he was a bad little boy. And Cassius'd say, "Oh Daddy, you don't know that little boy. He's badder'n we are!" I'd say, "Oh, no, he's better'n you all, and you all got to be good." And that'd make 'em be good boys. Trying to prove that he was better than that Jerry. OooooOoooooo, that used to make Cash mad at me! And he'd show me something bad that Jerry was doing, and I'd say, "Oh, no, he's a better boy than you." '

Young Clay's attitude toward money, like his distrust of Caucasians, was forced-fed into him by his father. He likes nothing better than to stuff the cash into his wallet and get out of town. 'I mostly save my money,' he said. 'I don't keep it in a bank. I have places where I just bury it.' His approach toward all financial institutions is one of suspicion. Years before, a reporter had tried to argue the point with Cassius, noting that banks insured by the government had become safe depositories. 'I don't want money in no bank!' Cassius insisted. 'I want it in real estate where I can point to a lot with an apartment on it and say, "There, that's mine." I want to be able to see it. I don't want *no* money in banks. The bank might burn down or something. And I don't want to have to worry about no stocks, or have a lot of investments and have to spend all my time checking on 'em.' He said his idea of financial security would be a fifty-unit apartment building – 'one for the poorer people, nothing fancy, so it'll always be filled. And at the end of each month I can go 'round and collect the rent and maybe make fifteen dollars on each apartment.'

Later, Cassius retreated even from those conservative ideas. 'I'm not buying much of anything these days,' he said in the early part of 1966, neatly managing to by-pass the fact that at that stage of his career he had no money with which to make purchases. 'I'm holding on to my money,' he said, ' 'cause things that cost twenty thousand dollars today you can get for ten thousand next year. Things that cost me a hundred thousand today I'll get it for forty thousand next year; so I just wait. I did buy two six-flat buildings in Chicago on the South Side. Nice buildings. One of 'em was just built, but I don't tell nobody where it's at because it's in a white neighbourhood and I don't want them to know I own it. I paid cash for both of those places, and one is valued at seventy-five thousand dollars, and the one that's valued at thirty-eight thousand I got for twenty-three thousand. I just paid cash outright for 'em. I got about a hundred thousand dollars' worth of real estate.' Since Cassius soon afterward came within a whisper of going to jail for failure to raise the money for court-ordered lawyer's fees, it must be assumed that his 'hundred thousand dollars' worth of real estate' was non-existent or else mortgaged to the limit.

The financial career of Cassius Clay became a succession of missed opportunities and bad investments. While he was refusing to avail himself of the business acumen of his sponsors, he was paying through the nose to buy his father a drinking spot in Louisville called 'The Olympic Club'. At first, it was a proud establishment, attracting a sporting clientele and bearing on the wall an inscription in fluorescent letters stuck on by the champion himself:

WORLD-HEAVY-WT.

●

CHAMIONSHIP
FLOYD-PATTERSON
v. s.
CASSIUS-CLAY.*
←19-62

It was only a matter of months before the elder Clay had managed to alienate customers and lose his son's investment. 'I couldn't handle it,' the father rationalised.

183

'I was afraid of something happening. After all, people was getting drunk there, see, and somebody liable to kill somebody, and I don't want that mark on me. Am I right? If somebody got killed, I'd be responsible, wouldn't I? Or I might be the first one that got killed.'

Early in young Clay's relationship with the Sponsoring Group, his handlers realised that the father's advice was the major menace to Clay's financial stability, and yet they could not exclude Senior from their negotiations: Cassius was still a minor.

'In the days when his father used to attend our finance meetings,' William Faversham recalled, 'we'd go through a bloody session after a fight. What we were trying to do was get Cassius to pay his taxes and sign the check for his fifteen per cent pension fund and pay back what he owed us – he was always into us for a healthy amount, forty, fifty thousand dollars – and this was a bloody, exhausting struggle, two or three hours, after every fight, with Mr Clay telling him that he couldn't get a square deal out of white men.'

'We had our biggest troubles over the pension fund,' said a member of the group's inner council. 'The original idea was that Cassius would put fifteen per cent of his share of every fight into a pension fund. The money would go to an outside, independent company that would invest it for him, and then when he was thirty-five, or when he quit boxing, either one, he'd have a nice nest egg. Well, we're sorry we ever mentioned the idea. The trust fund payment can be mutually waived, and he's constantly pressing us not to put money into it, and we're constantly pressing him to put it in. He has a perfect record and so do we: he has always voted not to put it in and we have always voted the opposite. Then we sit down and negotiate. We waived it a few times because his family needed the money or he needed it. I'd say that after all these years he's only got about fifty thousand dollars in the fund. If we had had our way, he'd have three or four times that much.'

'One day when we were discussing pension funds,' said Faversham, 'Mr Clay interrupted us and he said, "Look, there's one thing I don't need help on and that is investments. Nobody knows any more about investments than I do. I know all there is to know about investments. The only reason that I haven't got any money is I never had any money to invest." We all broke out laughing. One of the funniest remarks I ever heard!'

It fell to Gordon Davidson, the corporate tax lawyer who somehow found himself handling Clay's financial affairs on behalf of the sponsoring group, to do most of the talking at post-fight money meetings with the Clays, father and son. 'It was agony sometimes,' Davidson recalled. 'He'd take unreasonable financial positions on fights. He'd say, "That's not enough." He always wanted too much. He'd say, "A million people are gonna watch me, and this isn't enough money, it isn't enough money." He'd talk all these big figures: a hundred thousand, a million people, two million dollars, and then he'd come up and hit you for a loan somewhere on the road. And for how much? For twenty dollars, fifty dollars, something like that! We had a fund to cover this.'

'Yeh,' said a member of the group. 'We had a fund to cover it all right. We called it the theft fund. We knew we were gonna get hit and we knew we were never gonna get paid back. But it was never more than twenty-five, fifty dollars. Maybe sometimes ten dollars. It was just pocket money. Cassius is no deadbeat, understand. He likes to pay his bills. But if he hits you for a small amount, forget it. He doesn't consider that a loan. It's not the same to him.'

'He was always into us for big advances,' another member said. 'He'd take his after-tax money and *zip!* It'd be gone. He'd put it into his checking account and then it would go right out. On things like travel, clothes, automobiles, I don't know what all. One of the ways we advanced him money was paying his bills for him, and for his family. He used to call and say, "Put a thousand dollars in my mother's account." We'd keep a record. We used to buy him things like tyres, five dollars for this, ten dollars for that, one thousand, two thousand, three thousand. There'd be a long list maybe adding up to fifteen thousand dollars by the time we settled after a fight. And when it came time to settle, Clay'd say, "How much do I owe you?" and we'd say, "You owe us fifteen thousand seven hundred twenty-three dollars and twenty-seven cents," and hand him an itemised list. Never has he looked at that list or questioned anything on it! He'd just say, "Take that out! Now how much have I got?" He has a funny attitude about money, part penuriousness and part don't-give-a-damn.'

Cassius Jr's attitude on money matters can be evaluated by his handling of the purse from the first Liston fight in Miami Beach. 'We got paid in instalments,' Faversham said, 'and after one session I remember Cassius had forty thousand dollars coming to him. He went over to the Liberty Bank and asked for forty thousand-dollar bills. The bank sent for their president and of course they didn't have forty thousand-dollar bills. Who the hell does? 'I've never had a thousand-dollar bill in my life or even seen one. So they had to send to the Federal Reserve for it, and he walked out of the bank with forty thousand-dollar bills.'

Arthur Grafton, a senior partner in the distinguished Louisville law firm of Wyatt, Grafton and Sloss, remembered accompanying Clay to the bank after another such payoff. 'He had something like twenty-seven thousand dollars coming to him, I think it was,' said Grafton. 'That was what was left after he paid his divorce lawyers and a thousand dollars extra to a sparring partner and another five thousand somewhere else and whatever it was he owed us. We walked to the bank and he asked for twenty-seven thousand-dollar bills. The bank didn't have it, and Cassius said, "Well, how long would it take you to get it?" and the bank said about twenty minutes, from the Federal Reserve.

'Cassius said no, that'd take too long, and the tellers started making up his twenty-seven thousand in smaller denominations. We finally wound up with a great big pouch full of money, and on the side of it was written in big letters "First National Bank," and we had to carry that thing through the streets of Louisville to his hotel. Before we left, Cassius said to the lady teller: "You know, I'm gonna count this money back in my hotel room and you'll know it'll be an honest count because my lawyer will watch me." On the way back he was kidding me – I was nervous about this whole idea – and he said, "Do you think I'm gonna be held up? You do, don't you!" He said, "Maybe we should hire a cop. How much would it cost to hire a cop to walk back with us?" We got to the hotel and he spilled all the money out on the bed and started counting, and would you believe it? It was a thousand dollars short! We counted it five times and then carried the whole bag right back to the bank. They had already realised it was short and were expecting us. Then Cassius, twenty-seven thousand dollars in cash and all, flew off to Chicago.'

According to those who know Cassius best, the satchels of money he carries back to Chicago wind up in a checking account, but not before the champion has shown the money around town. 'He takes the bills and displays them for a while,' said a close friend. 'I know, 'cause I've seen him do it. He likes to feel it, run it through his fingers. When he first got into the big money, he used to settle with the income-tax people right after every fight, and he'd always get photostats right after every fight, and he'd always get photostats of how much he paid the government and then show the photostats to everybody.'

Despite all his wallet-choking paydays. Clay went broke except for the untouchable fifty thousand dollars in the trust fund tenaciously protected by the Louisville Sponsoring Group for his declining years. At his divorce hearing, Clay was asked where the money had gone. 'Seventy per cent goes to the government first,' he said. 'Then I help support my mother and father. Then I have a wife. I owe one thousand three hundred dollars on my wife's affairs. I paid some of that.' He said he had eight hundred dollars in a Chicago bank and fifty-two dollars in a Miami bank. 'I owe my lawyers,' he said, and looked around the room and started pointing at lawyers. 'I owe you. I owe him. I owe him. I owe everybody in this room.' How does a man who has earned a take-home pay approaching a million dollars manage to owe everybody? Said Gordon Davidson:

'The money just goes, and not to nefarious things. Like his divorce, that wasn't cheap. And he pays his personal lawyers a high retainer, a substantial amount. I can account for where seventy-five per cent of his money goes, and a lot of it is to personal lawyers. I won't tell you exactly where it goes, but you wouldn't be shocked at any of the expenditures.'

Insiders say that only a moderate percentage of Clay's money goes to the Muslim organisation as a church donation. And none of his money goes into flashy living – women, whisky, gambling and other such pleasures – as he is fond of pointing out. Indeed, in some ways Clay seems as penurious as the most conservative New England farmer. 'I'm not interested in clothes,' he says, and corroborates the remark by dressing like a high school senior on his way to a prom in a cheap rented dress suit, 'I just have enough clothes to keep going and be presentable. I used to have two suits, and now I only have five or six.' He brags that he has spent no money on a home of his own – 'I just live in hotels and do better things with my money, like buying a home for my mother and father in Louisville.' Nor is he a patsy who is an easy mark for borrowing friends, former friends and would-be friends. Once when he was with Huston Horn he put a dime in a jukebox and listened to Dee Clark sing 'Your Friends,' part of which goes: 'When you are down and out, there's not a friend in this world to help you out. But when you, when you get on your feet again, everyone will want to be your friend.'

Said Cassius: 'I like to sit here eating and wait for somebody to come up and want to borrow money. I don't have to wait long. They'll say, "Cassius, let me have ten till payday, my brother." I don't say nothing, just go over and play that record. Then the cat will say, "You trying to tell me something?" and I'll say, "Oh, no, my brother. I just wanted to hear that pretty tune. I think there's so much truth in the words, don't you?"'

Clay is absolutely impervious to bills presented to him when he is in the company of others. Once he invited a crowd of reporters to join him for dinner in a Miami restaurant, and quietly slipped the tab to one of the journalists. Then he left a five-dollar tip and remarked loudly: 'I always take care of my people!' The same victimised journalist was with Cassius some time later when the champion put the arm on him for a hundred dollars and said, 'I'll give it back to you in a week.' Several months later the newspaper man retrieved his hundred dollars, but only after pleading and finally using Angelo Dundee as a go-between to put pressure on Clay.

And then there are innumerable touches for two, three and five dollars, with none of his friends or acquaintances exempt from the honour. When I hardly knew Clay, and he in fact did not even know my name, I kept an interview rendezvous with him in the lobby of the Hampton House, a popular motel for Negroes in Miami. When I arrived, Clay was the centre of attention in the lobby, 'jiving' with his friends, as he explained. Quickly he detached himself and whispered to me: 'Man, you got any money?'

Having been forewarned of the possibilities, I said, 'A little.'

Cassius said, 'Well, I'm meeting somebody here at eleven and I want to buy 'em a present.'

We walked into the motel's gift shop, where Clay picked out a bottle of 'Tiger' aftershave lotion and allowed me to pay for it: $3.09. As we walked out, he spotted a friend walking in and he said to me: 'Quick. Gimme two dollars!' He handed the two bills to the newcomer and said to me, 'I'll pay you back tomorrow.' Tomorrow never came. Cassius justifies such minor hustles by the indisputable fact that journalists make money off him; so they should not mind a small amount of *quid pro quo*. On occasion he carries this attitude to the edge of reason and a little beyond. Once he threatened to conduct no more free interviews. 'If you want to talk to me,' he told reporters, 'it'll cost you three hundred dollars. Come on, form a line, three hundred dollars apiece and you can talk to the champion.' When the line failed to form, Cassius retreated from his ultimatum. Frequently in the course of extended interviews he threatened to charge the interviewer by the hour, but the Sponsoring Group and his own inner common sense always made him change his mind. Likewise, he adopted and then discarded a plan to give out no more free autographs. 'From now on,' he said, 'they is a dollar apiece.' He turns a dollar in any number of ways, including charging for his appearance at public events. At the behest of a Las Vegas motel, he showed up to help promote the second Patterson-Liston fight, and accepted five hundred dollars of gambling house money to throw around on the tables, so that the joint could take his picture and peddle his fame. 'Cassius threw the dice two or three times,' a friend recalls. 'Then he took the rest of the five hundred dollars and walked out. He'd lived up to the promise – he "visited the casino." But he wasn't gonna stand there and gamble his money away.'

Despite his money-grubbing and conservative personal habits, Clay found himself nearly penniless at the very point in his life when he had all but cut down the money tree by his remarks about the draft, and by the slow erosion of his box-office appeal. 'It wasn't so much that he threw his money around,' said a close friend, 'because he didn't. But what hurt him was that he didn't *use* the money he made. He didn't let his money make money. His investments, what few they were, they stunk. And in the meantime a billion people were moving in on him, living off him.'

Clay always required an expensive entourage, even back in his earliest years as a professional. Said Angelo Dundee: 'Whenever he used to fight out of town, these guys'd show up to see him, friends of his, and he'd put 'em up in his room. He'd have three, four guys lying around. One I remember was a soldier, built like a tank, and he'd come to every fight. There always was a half dozen guys come to every fight, a bunch of guys with us, always around us. The champ likes to be around people. He'd go batty in a regular isolated training camp.'

'That's an occupational hazard of being a fighter,' said Ferdie Pacheco. 'There are people who make a career out of hanging around boxers. They look for people like Cassius to come down the trail to zonk onto 'em. They did it to Sugar Ray Robinson. The fighters want these hangers-on; they serve a function, an entourage of lackeys and flunkies for which the fighters are duly paying. Cassius has one just like the rest of 'em had one.'

Cassius did not agree. 'I don't have many people around me,' he said. 'Just the people I employ. As far as hanger-ons, people who live wild party lives, flashy women, drinking wine and so on, I don't have that. My religious convictions keep me from all that, so I have all those people off of me.' His attitude seems to be that money spent on Muslims, on non-drinkers and non-smokers, is money well spent. Herbert Muhammad, son of the 'Messenger of Allah' himself, got three hundred dollars a week as business manager, and more when he became ring manager later. When Angelo Dundee was asked to describe Herbert's duties at pre-trial hearings in Clay's divorce action, he said, 'Herbert's business manager, that's all I know.' He was asked what Herbert did to earn thirteen hundred dollars while accompanying Clay on an exhibition tour in Europe. Angelo pondered and replied: 'Herbert helped put on the gloves.' A personal lawyer, also on the trip with Clay, earned a thousand dollars for his legal services. What legal services did he perform? Dundee did not have the answer to that question, but he did say: 'I know he helped. In the capacity over there he helped putting on the gloves for the sparring partners.' One of the most interesting items on the list of expenditures was a hundred dollars paid to Drew 'Bundini' Brown: for staying home.

At the Patterson fight, Clay carried his careless air about expenditures to an extreme, and managed to waste thousands of dollars that he sorely needed later. A member of his inner circle gave a graphic description of the *Arabian Nights* setting in Las Vegas:

'First off, two Egyptian broads turned up. I don't mean shriners, I mean real Egyptians, and they were his guests. My wife saw them in the lobby of the hotel and these two chicks were pegging the most expensive evening bags, a hundred-fifty, two hundred dollars each. They tagged them and put them on Clay's bill. Those saintly good ladies. . . . And they were down getting their hair done every day on his bill, too. If you had been in Vegas you wouldn't have believed what was going on in that hotel. He had those Muslims planted all over the place, at his own expense. One of 'em was in Clay's suite twenty-four hours a day. Clay had his penthouse and the thugs at the door cracking it like it was prohibition days, and *nobody* but coloured people getting in. Clay was picking up *all* the tabs, and the amount of hundred-dollar tickets that man gave away to Black Muslims, to anybody who showed up from any part of the country and said he was a Muslim, it was fantastic! One of the brothers would show up and Clay's flunky Muslim would say to Cassius, "Well, well, here's Brother so-and-so from Boston!" And Clay'd say, "How do you do, Brother so-and-so. We'll make sure you get two hundred-dollar seats."

'Now at the time of a fight a boxer's mind is usually on the fight. They walk as if they have a block of ice between them and the public. They're thinking about getting their heads knocked off. But not Cassius! He was walking around like an entrepreneur, walking around asking, "Who else hasn't got tickets? Who needs tickets? These two brothers right here, seat them up front!" And at the last minute, when the semi was on and Cassius still wasn't dressed, still lounging around in his robe, somebody says, "There's twenty-five brothers outside from Los Angeles, they can't get in." '

'So the promoter says, "It's a sell-out. There's no more seats. Where can we put 'em? The fire laws won't permit it." '

'Cassius said, "I don't care what the fire laws are and I don't care where you put them. Let 'em stand in the aisles. There's plenty of aisles to stand in the back." '

'The promoter says there's a law against that. So

Cassius began these thinly veiled threats that he won't go on. And by God, they let the twenty-five in, which then caused a hellacious riot. If you watch pictures of the fight, after a couple of rounds you'll see people standing up looking toward the back. It's the cops beating hell out of the Black Muslims because they would come and stand right in front of you. You'd be trying to see the fight and all you could see was some Black Muslim's rear end.'

The rapid infiltration of Clay's interests by the Black Muslims was watched with annoyance by some of the eleven members of the Louisville Sponsoring Group, and finally the indications were that the group was fed up with the champion. 'Clay has turned rancid,' said one member. 'It's no fun anymore. And there never was much money in it, by the time we paid those fancy expenses of his.'

By early 1966, Clay was hardly able to get a fight in the United States, and his already tangled financial affairs were thrown into a hopeless mess. His desperate need for dollars forced him into hurried bouts with the likes of George Chuvalo, who took punishment and dished it out like a marble statue, and Henry Cooper, one of whose claims to fame was that he had knocked Cassius down a few years ago with a right hand. Neither of these matches would have been made in normal times, but 1966 was not a normal year for the debt-ridden Cassius. He had based his financial future on two or three fat purses a year before the threat of military service loomed up to confuse the picture. He was committed to paying his ex-wife $15,000 a year for ten years and another flat payment of $22,500 to her lawyers, piddling sums for a heavyweight champion of the world but astronomical figures for a potential private in the Army. The legal bill was finally paid after a long palaver in which a judge threatened to throw the champion in the clink, but several other suits were brought against Clay. The humpty-dumpty fights against humpty-dumpty fighters relieved some of the pressure, but not all. And he faced the future with the very financial insecurity that the Louisville Sponsoring Group had worked so hard to avoid.

'I only plan to fight a year or so and then retire and be a minister of Islam,' said Cassius. 'That's the best thing I could do anyway. And then one day I'll get married and raise a nice family. I *got* to get married. I'm preparing for it all the time. I don't even have a home, because I'm doing wiser things with my money. I don't have nothing, except two cars. But when I get married I'll have a home like nothing you ever seen before.'

Clay skipped quickly over the matter of where he would raise the money for the palace he plans, but he figured he could hold the cost down to seventy-five thousand dollars by employing Muslim labour – 'We got carpenters and plumbers and everything I'd need.'

'My home'll be somewhere on the outskirts of Chicago and it'll be worth a hundred and fifty thousand dollars by the time I'm finished. I wouldn't buy a home that cost forty or fifty thousand dollars. If I had to pay that much I'd rather build something. The type I would like to build would be a one-storey with all glass on the front and on one side, like those modern motels you see, Holliday Inns, all glass that you can see through, and the rest solid granite stone for the other side and the back, with big picture windows out in the front and side and transparent glass on the other side and the back. Pretty, ain't it? And then I want a spacious big living room, one of the largest you can find, and I want nothing but goooooooold tweed carpet, the best carpet made. I priced it and it came to about eight thousand dollars. Hand-weaved. When the average person walks in it'll be like being in heaven, dreamland. And I'll have drapes, goooooooooold silk linings, satin shiny-colour drapes, and one of the living room walls will be mirrored with a big beautiful chandelier hanging down reflecting in the mirror, and a big beautiful living-room set in French provincional furniture and chairs, and one of these twenty-eight-hundred-dollar RCA Victor white TV sets with the big twenty-seven-inch screen.'

As Cassius talked on, I began to realise that this was one of the few times I had ever seen him take a clear and visible interest in what he was saying, as though he was talking about things that interested him and not things he felt he *should* be saying. His eyes flashed and the words came out easily and fluidly. This was not the way he discussed race, when his voice would take on a singsong quality, like a Southern Baptist preacher in a roadside church. Nor was this the way he discussed his own greatness, making long boring speeches that he had made so many times that they sounded sterile and canned. When Cassius talked about his pie-in-the-sky plan for his house, he was talking to please himself alone. The idea *thrilled* him, and he rattled ahead with a happy look on his face, like a little child explaining how he was going to have unlimited amounts of chocolate pudding when he grew to manhood. 'Then I will have a beautiful lonnnnnnnnnnnnnnnnnng U-shaped golden couch matching my rug,' he said, 'and then I will have a big glass on the wall, you can see through it like a windowpane, with a white background dug into the wall, sort of like you're looking into a fishbowl settin' sideways where the wall is cut out and it's all white. *Oh, don't you like the way we talking!* And inside it'll have all colours, pink and turquoise, coloured lights, lavender, blue, green, turquoise, and you can see the light but you can't see what's making the light.

'And then when I cut the lights out in my room and hook my recorder up – this is a new thing they've got –

as the music plays *boom boom boom ba boom boom ba boom ba boom ba boom* – the light changes. In my living-room walls I'm gonna have six little square block lights inset into the wall on both sides and every light will be fixed so it can change colour. So if I'm sitting in the dark and I push the turquoise colour the whole room is a purplish colour. I touch a soft yellow and the whole room is a soft yellow. I touch a gold and the whole room is gold. The fellow that owns the Astrodome in Houston has this, I saw it.

'And my whole living-room'll be seventy-five feet long, about half the size of the Fifth Street Gym. I want seven bedrooms, seven. I'm an international man. People come to see me from Arabia and Egypt, fans come by, and some might want to stay late. I'm a world figure where I'll always have somebody around me, and I'll have children one day. In my own bedroom I'll have a big long California-style bed. In another I'll have a king-size bed. In one we'll have a double bed. One will have a diamond-shaped bed. One will have a round bed. One will be an Asiatic Egyptian room. The walls'll be painted with the pyramids on them and the sphinx, in that standard brown desert colour, and the stars and the moons and camels on the desert. And one room will be my Japanese room, with the bed on the floor. And a colonial room, with a canopied bed. And an Indian-designed room with teepees, done real professional like, with real material like the real Indians used.

'And I'll have a basement as big as the house, and down there'll be about five more bedrooms for emergency in case some schools come to stay by my house, or lots of people. Then there will be an orange-juice bar, not a liquor bar, where it will come up to your knees and you'll have to reach down for the drink. That will be my latest design. You dig? My bartender will stand in a deep hole where he'll be standing at the level of the bar serving. I got the land for all this already. And there'll be another kitchen for picnics, in the basement, and they'll be cooking all the time there.'

One was reminded of Clay's father's grandiose schemes for 'Clay Kitchens' and 'Clay Enterprises' and all the pipe dreams of the future. Dreams sustain Cassius, and the more he is visited by adversity the more he retreats into dreams, some of them more fanciful than others. For example, he told about his aspirations as a fighter:

'Well, my goal now is to raise the world title to the universal title. Now I understand there are four billion people on earth, about four hundred million people, and out of four hundred million people we have about two hundred million men and out of two hundred million men I can't find one of these men to give me a good fight. Not one of these men to last a good round; so since there are two hundred million men on earth, and I can't find one to fight, I'm going to Cape Kennedy in 1969. A rocket ship will be leaving with two men. The first life will be leaving earth, I understand, leaving Cape Kennedy in 1969, going to Mars. They are now making preparations to build space stations between here and Mars to make the flight possible; so I hope to be in Cape Kennedy with the crown in 1969 and be on that ship to find contenders on other planets. There is life on Mars, but I understand that the ship takes seven months to get there, and if I leave in 1969 I shall arrive there in about 1970 and find the contender and bring four or five of these tall fellows back for title fights here in 1971. And to train for these people, I think Ernie Terrell, he's tall, six six, he will be a good warm-up in order to get used to fighting these men up there, and I'm going to also find Bill Russell. Wilt the Stilt Chamberlain, some of the tallest men we have here on earth, to train for these men because there are no more men on earth and

I really hope that – there's only one problem, they might not let me on that ship. I hope – I'm going to contact Martin Luther King and see if he can integrate those ships because they will send two men on the planet and I want to be the first coloured one.'

"You listen to stuff like that,' said a friend and admirer of the champion, 'and you know he's kidding. Then you listen a little more and you say to yourself, "I know he's kidding, but *am I sure?*" And after a while you hear him say so many things like that you figure at least part of the time he means it, no matter how nutty he sounds. 'Course, you never know with him – underneath everything else, he's quite a fox, that cat!'

There are some who wonder if Clay will still be champion by the time of his planned flight to Mars, and others who allow their wishful thinking to steer them toward a belief that Cassius is not a good fighter in the first place, and will lose his championship as soon as an adequate journeyman heavyweight comes down the road. To be sure, Clay has bad habits that would have cost a lesser man the championship years before. The worst of all his tendencies is his reluctance to take instruction from trainer Angelo Dundee, perhaps the wisest head in the business. At the Chuvalo fight in Toronto, Dundee said Clay 'listened a little,' but a steady stream of technical advice was shouted from Clay's corner by Sam Saxon, a man who knows as much about boxing as your Aunt Elonwy. 'The fact is Clay has no trainer or manager,' said a veteran member of the camp. 'You don't feel you're a trainer or a manager unless you correct your man's mistakes, unless he does what you're telling him. Clay don't listen to nobody no more. He always was bad about that, but now he's impossible.'

Cassius, at the outset of his pro career, was sent to San Diego to study under the master, Archie Moore, but before a few weeks had gone by, Moore was on the telephone to Bill Faversham: 'I think I'm gonna have to ask you to take the boy home. My wife is crazy about him, my kids are crazy about him and I'm crazy about him, but he just won't do what I tell him to do. He thinks I'm trying to change his style, but all I'm trying to do is add to it.'

Faversham told Archie that Clay needed a spanking. 'He sure does,' Moore said, 'but I don't know who's gonna give him one, including me.'

A few years later, one of Clay's sparring partners, a heavy hitter himself, tried to get Cassius to improve his defences. 'I said to him, "Champ, pull your left hand in, it's out too far." He looked at me and he said, "I got my own style. Nobody tells me nothing." Then I hit him with a beautiful left hook, and I told him, "Listen, you know why I hit you? 'Cause I want to teach you a lesson to keep your hands up." And then he tells me, "You come on do it again. Just keep boxing! Don't tell me how to box." So I hit him with another beautiful left, I never will forget it. But it didn't teach him nothing!'

To be sure, Angelo Dundee was able to bring refinements to Clay's style, but the lessons were taught the hard way, by indirection and applied psychology, and it is doubtful that another trainer would have had the patience. 'He thinks he's done everything himself,' Angelo said, 'and that's fine with me, and if you look at it his way, he's right. All I did was suggest. You can't handle him the way you do the usual fighter. You don't regiment him. He had enough of that. You just have to use indirection. He never used to have the left jab he has now. A daily nicking at his pride did it. He'll be the last guy in the world to admit that anybody did it but him, but that doesn't bother me. He didn't have a left uppercut; he's got one now. He was throwing a left jab, but it was a slap. It had no authority. He would keep his left knee up. Now you'll see when he throws a left jab his left knee is bent. Gives him leverage, distance; he *reaches* you. But you have to show him things like that slowly. Up until a few fights ago he never hit a speed bag. It took me that long to teach him this was good for his reflexes, his rhythm.'

'Clay has fought a series of fights with a number of boxers who were not really in the same class as himself', said one of his critics. 'And this is all to Angelo's ever-lasting credit as a matchmaker. Angelo is a great judge of opponents, how they're going over the hill, when they're going over the hill, what style meshes with Clay's style, when to avoid a guy and when to break your neck to get a fight with a guy. That's the element that makes a great manager. That's what made Jack Hurley and that's what made Cus D'Amato. Everybody knows about them but nobody thinks about Angelo because Clay's got everybody buffaloed into thinking he was so great he could have licked anybody with or without Angelo's help. Picking out the right man for your guy – Angelo's never been given enough credit for that. Clay beat a bunch of name TV guys who were just over the hill, and nobody knew they were except Angelo.'

Said Ferdie Pacheco, who has watched the situation from the inside for six years, 'It's a very awkward situation for Angelo, and only somebody of his temperament could handle it. Doc Kearns or any of those old-timers would have been buried by it. I mean all the times Angelo's had to handle that pack of Muslims that follows Clay around. Now, Angelo's got enough great fighters so he doesn't need to take all this baloney. But he's really handled those people nicely, to the point of almost being obsequious and yet firm enough to maintain his own dignity. He's had some tough times with them. These people around Cassius, they'd say, "We're intelligent, we can read and write, we're the top of the heap," and then about two minutes later one of 'em would say,

"Who's gonna get the plane reservations to get out of here?" And before you know it there's eighteen people in Angelo's room saying "Get me out on the two o'clock plane." He's got to do all that. Here he is handling the world heavyweight champion and he has to spend time doing paperwork worrying about where people are sitting. Every minute somebody is hitting town and presenting a new problem for him. I never saw anybody work as hard as Angelo has at some of these fights. He's done a fantastic job, and I don't know whether Cassius truly appreciates it. He's a little gruff at times with Angelo.'

'Angelo has been a miracle man with Clay,' said another member of the Clay Establishment, 'but not even Angelo is gonna be able to save the championship for that kid. Angelo can't get him to raise his guard. He can't get the kid to cut out that show-off footwork that makes him look like a big Chuck Davey, makes him waste an awful lot of energy that he's not always gonna have. He can't get the kid to cut out this foolin' around in the ring: tapping the other guy on the top of the head, leaning in with his head, stupid stuff like that. Angelo knows all this, but Angelo's the most loyal guy alive. He says, "How can you argue with success? This kid became champion of the world." And I say, "Yeh, the kid became champ because he's got moves like a welterweight and a hell of a God-given talent and because there's nobody around to test him." But what's gonna happen when he loses some of that edge? When he loses that extra tenth of a second that he has now? He'll stick out that big chin of his and some quick young kid on the make'll pop him one. He'll lose that championship 'way before he should, that's what'll happen, and the sad thing about it is if he'd listen to Angelo, and start fighting like a mature human being, he could be champion for ten more years.'

Said the loyal Angelo: 'Listen, this kid is only twenty-four years old. He won't even mature till he's twenty-six or twenty-seven and he's not about to lose that championship. People say he should take my advice more. Well, I got carried away by some of those guys talking about how his hands are too low and so forth and I got to thinking maybe it's wrong, let me get his hands up there, and I did it once and he took my advice and he was so ineffectual he was horrible. It was in the Doug Jones fight. He put his hands up in the second round because he got nailed by that right hand earlier and I said, "Get your hands up there." And he was terrible! This is not him. Now I leave him alone on things like that. Maybe when he gets older he'll have to learn to fight with his hands up. But hands down is right for now. He doesn't have to listen to me about that. And on the things that really count – well, he listens to me enough.'

It is a simple axiom of boxing that the older a fighter gets, the less he can rely on natural assets and the more he begins to lean on his trainer's advice, on finesse and conditioning and know-how instead of the raw skills of youth. Angelo Dundee's protestations withstanding, Clay is listening to him hardly at all, and taking no advice whatever from others who could help him. Pacheco, who knows enough about boxing and conditioning to qualify as a trainer himself, recalled a talk with Clay before the Patterson fight: 'I was afraid he had some kind of plan like keeping the fight going to punish Patterson, in his usual Crusades way of thinking. And so I said to him in the dressing room, "All you owe the public is the best fight you can make and if that takes sixty seconds that's what it takes. If it takes a minute and sixty seconds, *that*'s what it takes. Go out and do the best you can and knock this guy out fast. Don't fool around with him because he's got a good hook and he's still capable of throwing it."

'And he just calmly looked at me and he said, "I don't have to listen to what you're telling me. God has already told me what to do." About that time I started realising that there were whistles going off someplace and I said to myself, "Okay, don't interfere. He's hearing from the outer world."'

'Cassius is not a truly bad person,' Pacheco said. 'He's a misguided person at worst. I remember when he first came here to Miami to train. He was pretty much unspoiled. It was as if they'd taken a can and opened it up and out came this eighteen-year-old well-proportioned guy with his childish ideas of fame and fortune. He would tell me he was looking for the day when he'd have a great big home on top of a hill and three great big Cadillacs. And he was going along unconfusedly toward those goals till the Muslims got him. He was heading toward a Cabin-in-the-Sky type of world, plenty to eat, everything for his mother and father, a new house, a car for him, a car for his brother, a car for his aunt, everybody's gonna get a car.

'Now I can't honestly tell you what the prognosis is. He's got to live in the world of coloured people, and they don't like him. It's an amazing thing, but they don't. They've been saying don't make waves for so long, and here comes a guy splashing around in the pool. They're saying, "Shut up already! Things are getting better. What are you gonna set us back for?" Cassius will just have to mature. It's not impossible. Some men mature late in life and some men mature in adversity. And boy! is he heading full-speed into adversity! For one thing, he's got to win every fight from now on either by a knockout or by a big margin. Remember, if any boxer can stand on his feet for fifteen rounds against Clay in an American ring, why, the American public is so desirous of lancing this boil on their rear end that they just might lance him right out of the decision. They may give him the old zinger, boxing-style. That's one of the adversities he faces: going into the Army as the ex-champion of the world.'

Sometimes Cassius sounds as though he would not mind becoming the ex-champion of the world, as though the crown might be weighing heavily on him. Once he was asked if he thought ex-fighters missed the ring. 'If his life is based around showing off and if his life is based around being seen and seeing,' Cassius said, inadvertently describing himself perfectly, 'then I would say when it is time for him to quit he would miss it. But if he had nothing else to fall on, if nothing bigger is in his mind, if this is all he can see, then it do hurt him to have to go to places and watch people not asking for autographs, watch the crowd roaring and shouting and jumping and looking for other fighters. Then that might hurt him, but I am a man who don't care. And when I am through I can say I have had my fun. I have seen the world. I have earned the most that I could earn, and I can't stay forever. I mean I am a human. I have to go sometime. And I am so tired of publicity and things and people mobbing you and you have no freedom. You don't belong to yourself, you know? You don't own yourself. Everybody's watching you. I'm glad when the day come when I can walk around and not be noticed and all of this.'

'Yeh,' said Angelo Dundee, 'that's what he says now, but he'll *hate* it when it's all over. He'll go batty. He loves to be in front of people. The ring and the gym, they're his stage. He's like a guy going to the Academy Award dinner when he's receiving the Academy Award every day! This is the thrill he gets. He's happy when he's performing for people. He's not just like any ordinary fellow, you know. When he's gone there'll never be another one like him.'

Cassius, drawing on his background of time and stars

and 'spooky-mindedness,' is capable of taking a lyric view of the future, of sounding like a slightly unpolished twentieth-century Ecclesiastes. 'Everything is based on time,' he once said. 'I mean you take a mother when she's having a child. It takes nine months for the child to be birth. That's time. It takes time. Will man go to the moon or not? We don't know. It takes time. You take the earth we're living off, for example; it takes time for the earth to rotate around the sun, and in that time a change takes place. Now if we notice in the winter-time things are dead. You're in the house. You don't want to go out, your mind changes. Time changes things. The trees. You look out the window. You don't see no life on the trees. They're dead. The snow is *that* deep. People are running. Your mind changes. We go through a change just like the seasons do. As soon as summer-time comes, you put on your T-shirt, you run out to see the birds, the flowers are blooming and your mind changes. ... You're happy. You're walking your dog in the park. The grass is green, the flowers are blooming. But you wouldn't just go out and shoot yourself because the time of the seasons are at its dead stage like right now. In a few more months it'll be nice and gay out there. So you wouldn't just say, "Man, it's cold out there, or can't go nowhere, I can't walk my dog, there ain't no flowers," and shoot yourself.' Cassius Marcellus Clay paused. 'You wait,' he said. 'It takes time, and then the flowers will bloom.'

Appendix

HOW GOOD IS CASSIUS CLAY THE FIGHTER AND HOW does he compare with the other heavyweight champions? 'He's as good as any of 'em and he can be champ as long as he wants to be,' said Angelo Dundee. 'The only guy that can lick him is himself: by not getting properly conditioned for a fight, by taking a guy too cheap, by not having the proper attitude. So far he's been right for every fight. People think he'll tend to get fat and out of condition and lose the championship. Maybe so, but never because of conditioning. People don't understand that the champ is very vain when it comes to his body. He knows he must get his body svelte for every fight, because all those people're gonna be looking at him. Now he's gonna work hard to do that, and when he's working hard to make his body beautiful, he's getting into condition. You can't show me anybody in boxing today that boxes as many rounds as the champion does before a fight.'

'These are my tools,' Cassius said, pointing to his legs and his arms. 'A good mechanic keeps his tools clean. I keep my teeth clean. I keep my body clean. I keep my hands clean. I keep my tools sharp and clean. A good eye doctor know where his tools are, and I know where my tools are. I keep 'em clean and sharp. I keep every muscle I got sharp. I even do toe exercises. That's why

I'm so bouncy for my size. My backers owns a jewel. I am a jewel. I am a clean and sparkling champion.'

Ferdie Pacheco, despite his down-to-earth unglamorised view of Cassius, sees him as a skilled practitioner of the art of boxing. 'You have to admit that the man is a polished fighter now,' the doctor said. 'He's getting to the point where you can recognise he's a good fighter. He's got the speed of a welterweight, fast hands, fast reflexes, a long, tall body. But it's also true that he's never been challenged properly. He's still doing a lot of wrong things, but he's doing them in an era when there's nobody to contest it.'

At the other extreme Clay has several harsh critics. Ingemar Johansson sparred with Clay several years ago. According to onlookers, Clay, then an unranked fighter, gave the Swede a boxing lesson. Perhaps the memory rankled. Said Ingo: 'I went one round with him in Convention Hall in Florida when I was training, but otherwise I haven't seen too much of him. At that time, during the round in Florida, I didn't think he could do anything. He was a nothing. He must have improved but I still think he's a nothing. He's too weak and he can't punch. He just talks too much. Maybe he will have more power when he's older. I really can't find any good points.'

Said Dr Alexander Robbins, Miami Beach Boxing Commission physician who was slightly hoaxed by Cassius before the first Clay-Liston fight: 'Cassius is no Jack Dempsey. He's getting away with a lot 'cause there's no competition, no one around to give him a beating. A good boxer, a good slugger, would set him on his ass. Did you ever see a good fighter back away with his chin, the way Cassius does? A good fighter'll go in, get his chin low and go in. But when you back away with your chin sticking out, one little clip and you're a dead duck. Someone's gonna clip Clay's wings, surely. Jack Dempsey would have put him away with one punch. Rocky Marciano would clobber him to death. But he has no one to fight.'

The most restrained and balanced view of the un-defeated champion comes from the Madison Square Garden crowd, the old heads around New York who watched him come in and out of town for some half-dozen years. Said Nat Fleischer, editor of *The Ring*:

'He is one of the cleverest boys we've had since Gene Tunney and Billy Conn were in their heyday. Clay un-questionably has more speed than any other fighter in the history of the division – no heavyweight could approximate his quickness. However, as a hitter Clay doesn't rate. It is for this reason that I cannot rank him amongst the first fifteen heavyweight champions.

'You can't fault his courage; otherwise he wouldn't have taken on Liston who, if you will remember, was universally accepted as a killer at the time Clay took the title from him. Despite this, he falters when he's hit hard. Clay especially does not like to be punched to the head.

'His speed and his jab are Clay's two great assets, but he must settle down. He must take his work more seriously. Perhaps he could become in time a more powerful hitter. He certainly is big enough and he has the raw power and the structure to be a hitter. But right now he hops around too much. He should learn to plant himself before throwing punches. That would be the first step toward getting power.

'Still in all, he is young and probably it is unfair to make a permanent judgment yet. But the boy champion is now a man and I doubt that he will change. More to the point, I doubt that he *can* change.'

Said Teddy Brenner, Madison Square Garden pro-moter: 'Cassius Clay is the best heavyweight of his era, but his era – let's remember – hasn't been much. Off-hand I don't think Clay would have stood a chance against Joe Louis. Joe would have gotten to him eventually. Louis had an old saw: "They can run but they can't hide," and that would have proved out.

'I don't sell Clay short. He has unquestionably the best speed and reflexes of any heavyweight to tie on a pair of gloves, but he does not have a heavyweight punch – at least not a punch of championship calibre. Louis and Marciano could pull out a fight in the fifteenth round or at least late in the fight, as Joe did against Billy Conn in the first fight, knocking him out in the thirteenth round. And Marciano was far behind in his title fight with Walcott and then knocked him out in the thirteenth round to win. This is something Clay could never do. He just doesn't have that kind of punch.

'Frankly, I think Clay would have had life and death with a clever boxer like Walcott, who could also punch. And there's no way that Clay could have beaten Ezzard Charles. Forget Floyd Patterson and Ingemar Johansson, Clay would have taken both of them on their best nights. As far as Liston's concerned, the jury's still out.

'Yet it's hard to be too critical of Clay. It's early in his career and he has yet to be tested. I would like to see him in with a clever boxer like Zora Folley and somebody like Ernie Terrell, whom he wouldn't outsize. A big puncher like Cleveland Williams would be another yardstick, but who knows if Williams can come back after being shot in the gut? I do know that a Doug Jones, a fighter with fast hands, gave Clay an awful time and he had trouble with Billy Daniels, a big stick with a left hand. I can't forget that Cassius won the title from a strange Sonny Liston and at the time Liston quit, the fight was tied three rounds apiece.

'I personally would have liked to have seen Clay have more fights, better grounding, before he won the title. As it is, when he begins to lose some of his speed – and he'll start to slow down within the next year or so – what can he use for defence?'

Said another veteran Madison Square Garden promoter, Harry Markson:

'Cassius Clay is a fighter of marked ability. He has many of the attributes of a great athlete: he's a superb boxer, well conditioned, a fighter of stamina who recovers quickly from a damaging punch. Too, he throws punches in relentless combinations. Summing it up, he knows how to fight. Unfortunately, the complete picture of the complete fighter is missing. His punching prowess is in doubt. For this reason he is not in the same class as the great champions of my own era, from the mid-thirties till now.

'I personally don't like to rate fighters of different eras. I think the best that could be said – or should be said – is that Clay is the best fighter of his time. He is certainly that. Cassius Clay has done everything that has been asked of him. He has fought everyone and has ducked no one. Certainly there is not a heavyweight since Marciano that Clay would not have beaten. In fact, Clay and Marciano would have been an interesting match: a title fight between two undefeated fighters. And Clay might well have won the fight.

'Rocky was tough and very capable, but he cut easily, and this might have been too much of a handicap. Yet Clay would have been disadvantaged since he doesn't fight inside and this is where Marciano fought best. In close, he would unloose powerful hooks that might well have been too much for Cassius. If Rocky could have hurt Clay with hooks, then Joe Louis would have killed him with the same punch. The critics write lavishly about Clay's jab, but Joe's was even better. He'd knock fighters out with a jab and this is something Clay cannot do. Joe's right was equally as powerful and that's why he was so dangerous.

'Clay is not in Louis' class, this can be safely said. But, then, Louis was the best-schooled fighter I ever saw, and lack of schooling is Clay's biggest failing. He is just not well schooled. Not that you can necessarily fault him for it. If there were more fighters around and he had had more fights before he won the title, then he might have rated among the all-time great fighters. As it is, he falls short of this standing.'

Said Nat Loubet, managing editor of *The Ring*: 'As a defensive fighter Clay ranks with the best. He is perhaps the equal of Jack Johnson in this aspect of fighting. But his ability to punch or to take a punch remains in doubt. He has the fastest hands and feet in heavyweight history and he is truly a magnificent boxer. But in this division hitters reign and at hitting Clay is out of his class. Dempsey would have taken him with his one-two punch and Louis' volleys would have accomplished the same result.

'Tunney and Clay would have been a good match: two skilful boxers and Clay would have stood a good chance of winning. Max Baer would have been an interesting opponent, but I believe Max would have been discouraged by Clay's jab, which is incredibly fast and altogether a formidable weapon. Schmeling would never have seen Clay, so forget him. Walcott-Clay would have been a hell of a fight. Charles, himself an accomplished boxer with exceptional combinations, would have beaten Clay.

'Clay and Marciano would have been a brawl. I think Clay would have cut him to pieces and beaten him. Archie Moore was just too slow, he didn't stand a chance. Outside of Willard and Carnera, Clay has the longest reach of any heavyweight champion. And he knows how to use it. He is by far the fastest man to wear the crown, but not faster than Joe Louis with his hands. Louis was in a class by himself. He had an explosive punch and Clay doesn't, and that's the big chink in Clay's ability.

This is the reason that you cannot rate him with the great champions of the division. He is not a big puncher in a division where power is the dominant criterion.'

Said Jimmy Jacobs, producer of fight films (one of which, alone of all the pictures taken, showed conclusively that Clay's knockout of Sonny Liston in their second fight was not on a phantom punch): 'I don't believe Clay has reached his peak; so it is very difficult to evaluate his eventual standing properly. I know he was better in Toronto against George Chuvalo than he ever was before, and I suspect he's still several years away from his best performance. Clay's great strength is his unbelievable elusiveness. This is an attribute that is unique in the heavyweight division. Even a welterweight would have difficulty hitting him.

'Another of his qualities is his magnificent conditioning. Like Rocky Marciano, Clay always comes into the ring in superb fighting trim. Clay has one of the qualities – perhaps the most important one – that made Louis a great champion: His competitive spirit is exceptional. On five different occasions, Clay has been belted to the canvas only to get up and win the fight. This is a very significant attribute and one that the press is reluctant to grant him.

'And he truly believes that he is the best heavyweight in the world. This is an unaccountable plus. When everything else is equal, Clay inevitably will be the winner because he knows he is the better man.

'Unquestionably, Clay – along with Louis – has the best left jab in the history of the division. Some of the critics grudgingly acknowledge this, but they deny his punching power. Let me put myself on record: I am a believer. Clay is unquestionably a puncher. His knockout ratio rivals that of Marciano. He destroys everyone he meets, but in his own way. He chops and cuts them down instead of crumpling his opponents with one heavy punch. Perhaps he is capable of heavy punching, too, but he doesn't try.

'Early in his career, Clay made a very important decision: he figured that with his elusiveness and speed no one was going to hurt him so long as he stuck to his style, which was to hit and move and stay constantly on his toes. And no one has! As a result, he seldom sets himself to punch. But with his tremendous strength he still is able to put power into his blows, even when he is on his toes.

'To date, there have been twenty-three heavyweight champions, and of the twenty-three I would rate Clay third – Joe Louis, Rocky Marciano and then Clay. I put him ahead of Jack Dempsey, because if you analyse Dempsey's record you will see that he couldn't handle the truly exceptional boxer like Tunney. Clay is not only a brilliant boxer and ring tactician, but he is a first-rate puncher besides. Clay might even have taken Marciano, although I have my doubts. Rocky was almost impossible to hurt and his conditioning and drive were so impressive that I have to believe he would have got to Clay eventually. Marciano did cut, and Clay punches with twist, and this has the effect of cutting men – Liston is a good example – who never cut before. At any rate, it would have been a good battle and Marciano would have been only a slight favourite.'

CASSIUS CLAY — PROFESSIONAL BOXING RECORD

Date	Opponent	Location	Result
October 29, 1960	Tunney Hunsaker	Louisville	Decision in 6 Rounds
December 27, 1960	Herb Siler	Miami Beach	TKO in 4 Rounds
January 17, 1961	Tony Esperti	Miami Beach	TKO in 3 Rounds
February 7, 1961	Jim Robinson	Miami Beach	TKO in 1 Round
February 21, 1961	Donnie Fleeman	Miami Beach	TKO in 7 Rounds
April 19, 1961	Lamar Clark	Louisville	KO in 2 Rounds
June 26, 1961	Duke Sabedong	Las Vegas	Decision in 10 Rounds
July 22, 1961	Alonzo Johnson	Louisville	Decision in 10 Rounds
October 7, 1961	Alex Miteff	Louisville	KO in 6 Rounds
November 29, 1961	Willie Besmanoff	Louisville	TKO in 7 Rounds
February 11, 1962	Sonny Banks	New York	KO in 4 Rounds
February 28, 1962	Don Warner	Miami Beach	TKO in 4 Rounds
April 23, 1962	George Logan	Los Angeles	TKO in 4 Rounds
May 19, 1962	Billy Daniels	New York	TKO in 7 Rounds
July 20, 1962	Alejandro Lavorante	Los Angeles	KO in 5 Rounds
November 15, 1962	Archie Moore	Los Angeles	KO in 4 Rounds
January 24, 1963	Charlie Powell	Pittsburgh	KO in 3 Rounds
March 13, 1963	Doug Jones	New York	Decision in 10 Rounds
June 18, 1963	Henry Cooper	London	TKO in 5 Rounds

215

February 24, 1964	Sonny Liston	Miami Beach	TKO in 7 Rounds
May 25, 1965	Sonny Liston	Lewiston	KO in 1 Round
November 22, 1965 •	Floyd Patterson	Las Vegas	KO in 12 Rounds
March 28, 1966	George Chuvalo	Toronto	Decision in 15 Rounds
May 21, 1966	Henry Cooper	London	TKO in 6 Rounds
August 6, 1966 •	Brian London	London	KO in 3 Rounds
September 10, 1966	Karl Mildenberger	Frankfurt	TKO in 12 Rounds
November 14, 1966 •	Cleveland Williams	Houston	TKO in 3 Rounds
February 6, 1967 •	Ernie Terrell	Houston	Decision in 15 Rounds